Dear Jim

REFLECTIONS ON THE
BEAUTY OF ANGLING

To Regina

Dear Jim

REFLECTIONS ON THE
BEAUTY OF ANGLING

Alexander Schwab

MERLIN
UNWIN
·BOOKS·

First published by Merlin Unwin Books (Ludlow, UK) in 2004

ISBN 1 873674 791

Design and production by
        Matthew Lloyd at Think Graphic Design, Ludlow.
Printed and bound by
        Cambridge University Press, UK.

Contents

Acknowledgements

Many people have assisted in one way or another in the preparation of this book and I would like to thank every one of them. I would like to thank especially David Cleaver and friends from the Swindon Angling Centre, Jo and Peter Warner from the Ivy House Lakes in Grittenham (Wiltshire), the Peer family (and Noé) and Kurt Wüst for their spontaneous last minute help. Likewise many thanks to Joseph Lipartiti from La Boutique du Pêcheur, Geneva, and Yvan Marcato also from Geneva, and the Burger family from Lutry. Urs Bernhard and his team from Fischereiartikel Bernhard in Wichtrach have been most helpful. Bryn Hammond, author of the seminal *Halcyon Days*, has given me important last minute tips on current angling literature. My friends Roland Henrion (saltwater fly fishermen should look up his website www.smartfisher.com) and Roland Wüthrich have been assisting in various ways. Professor James D. Rose, University of Wyoming, has advised on the pain issue and Professor David Oderberg, University of Reading, had an eye on the philosophical content. Karen and Merlin Unwin and their team must be the best publishers an author can wish for. My wife, Regina, contributed not only many excellent ideas but also encouraged me all the way.

The people mentioned above do not necessarily share my views, nor is anyone other than me responsible for any errors.

Alexander Schwab
Biglen, Switzerland
March 2003

The leaping trout sees
far below, a few white clouds
as they flow.

Onitsura (1660–1738)

fishing

Send Chat Attach Address Fonts Colors Save As Draft

To: alex@philosofish.ch

Cc:

Subject: fishing

Dear Alex,

In class today we talked about fishing. I said that I enjoyed it. Some of my classmates seemed quite shocked and went on about cruelty, the poor fish on the hook and so on. We discussed it for a while and I ended up having to write a paper "What's good about fishing?" Can you give me some ideas, please?

Love,
Jim

Receive

THE CENTRE OF THE UNIVERSE

Dear Jim,

Why start at the beginning when you can go straight to the heart of the matter? The centre of the universe is *The Lobster* in Waterville. If you have any doubt about that, then ask the anglers who congregate there after a long day. *The Lobster* is a hothouse where the horizons of piscatorial knowledge are expanded on a daily basis. Daring hypotheses are aired with Guinness-fuelled conviction, only to be mercilessly crushed by the facts the following day. Wild speculation then resolve about the right fly, can make all the difference to the next fishing session. Wisdom is offered and eagerly sought, with stories of great angling feats and curious incidents, many of which generate lasting astonishment and at least temporary knowledge. This discursive style – some would say method – characterises the science of angling and accounts for the fact that all angling knowledge seems to be genteelly frayed at the edges. *The Lobster*, like thousands and thousands of pubs the world over, is not only a noble institution for the advancement and dissemination of angling knowledge but, of course, also a refuge for the dispirited and a stage for celebrations. There the roles can change within a day: today's downcast angler can be tomorrow's comforter.

The Lobster is not exclusively an angler's pub. It is a busy haunt frequented by locals and tourists alike. Waterville, situated at the south-western tip of Ireland, is also famous these days for its golf course, but its place in world history originates in "The River", "The Butler Pool" and "Lough Currane" renowned for its sea trout. Among other world-famous figures, Charlie Chaplin regularly visited Waterville for its fishing and to this day you might meet the odd celebrity – including a mysterious Indian prince – wetting a line. A special tradition in *The Lobster* is the display of the day's catch in the pub. The fish, salmon or sea trout, are placed on special silver plates to be marvelled at by all. A little note explains the who, when and with what. This archaic show draws complete strangers into conversation with each other more than any art exhibition could ever do. It is also, of course, conducive to business. The lucky anglers feel rightly obliged to buy a few pints, which in turn provokes a few more rounds and so on. The "so on" is a sort of conservation measure, because the following day's fishing begins later than usual and concentration and reflexes tend to be on the slack side.

The initial reaction to a fish on display is a moment of respectful wonderment. After that has passed, one can distinguish two groups of admirers: the anglers will gaze longingly at the fish and you can all but see their thoughts racing; the non-anglers will often ask "What is it?" and contemplate the fish more like one would a picture or a statue. However, angler and non-angler will eventually come to the same concluding statement, which is more often than not an appreciative comment: "That's a fine fish". Or a "nice", "lovely" or a "great" fish.

A fresh-run salmon is a shining, perfectly proportioned glory and the embodiment of one of nature's most fascinating secrets. Such a fish will elicit more than "fine" or "great". Beauty will be called upon to express a mix of facts and feelings: "Now, that's a beautiful fish" or "What a beauty" or "That's the most beautiful fish I've ever seen".

There's a truth about that salmon lying there on that silver plate which is never seen when, for example, the netters unload masses of fish. The netted salmon is a commodity, a product. Netting fish is anonymous: a hundred salmon in a net mean nothing; there is absolutely nothing there that elevates those salmon and the fishermen to the status of the salmon caught with rod and line. To begin with, the angler's salmon is associated with skill and personal achievement. No salmon hauled in with a net will inspire the same admiration as the salmon caught with rod and line. The salmon at the fishmonger's can be a fine fish, a good fish, a lovely fish, an excellent fish but it can never be a beautiful fish like the one on the silver plate. The story of the angler, the story of the fish, the story of when and how the fish took the angler make all the difference. So there is something more to beauty than just the object.

That something is the main theme of my letter to Jim. He caught his first fish at the age of eight on holiday with his brother, Sam, and his parents. It was a whitefish, on Switzerland's most beautiful body of water, Lake Thun, which is my home fishing ground. The whitefish (coregonus sp.) is a cousin of the trout and cruises this lake in search of food, i.e. chironomid larvae (bloodworms), emergers of all sorts, and the like. You fish for it at a likely spot from an anchored boat. You use a feather-light rod with a very, very fine tip. The main line is braided, and the attached leader is a paternoster rig with five nymphs and a lead weight. You lower this to the appropriate depth and then you gently, gently lift your rod, always watching the tip. At the slightest of pulls you strike. The take of the big whitefish is almost imperceptible: many takes you don't feel at all, you can only see them. Good whitefish anglers fish "on sight only" and consistently catch more fish than those relying on feeling. This sounds not much of a challenge but once you try it you discover that there is more to it than meets the eye. Anyway, I had instructed Jim and in contrast to other boys and girls of relatives and friends I had on the boat, he

was absolutely cool about it. His enthusiasm didn't fizzle out; there was no "Alex, where are they?" after five minutes, nor any of that barely contained fidgeting after a while, when nothing happens. I didn't even need to entertain him to keep his mind from wandering. He was so quiet and concentrated at his end of the boat that I forgot him until he announced in a matter-of-fact voice, "I've got one", upon which I turned round and stupidly asked, "You what?" I was amazed: there he was playing his first fish with aplomb while I was getting more excited than he was. We netted and killed the prize. Then, as Jim's concentration relaxed, a big, big smile appeared on his face – a smile expressing an unashamed sense of achievement, pride, happiness, optimism (I've got the hang of this. Bring 'em on!) and joy all rolled into one unique moment of glory!

Jim caught two more fish that day and I also got a couple; this was going to be a red-letter gala-dinner day. When it was time to reel in, I said to Jim that he should carry on fishing while I cleaned the fish. Again he surprised me by insisting that he deal with his fish himself. So I showed him how to do it and again he applied himself to the job with extraordinary concentration and thoroughness, addressing the various tasks involved systematically and unhurriedly. There was simply no way that boy would cut himself with the razor-sharp knife. He showed the same adroitness in all things fishing. Wide awake the whole day, on the way back the hero fell asleep in the car. He was so exhausted he wouldn't wake up when we arrived back home. His father lifted him out of the seat and then set him in a deck chair in the garden, intending to wake him up for dinner. Come dinner, Jim was still in Morpheus' arms, and the parents decided not to wake him up. The Jim-transport-caravan moved up the stairs to his room (we kept his fish for him until the next day). The next day, Jim was twice as hungry as usual and finished breakfast twice as fast while the adults lingered on twice as long over a cup of tea. This was taxing Jim's patience too much. He asked for permission to leave the table, went to the porch and came back with the car key. With a great theatrical gesture he slammed it on the table, looked at me reproachfully and urged me impatiently, "Come on Alex, come on!"

Jim doesn't go fishing these days: he now casts his line for girls. Nevertheless, fishing unexpectedly re-entered his life. Jim had gone for a soft-option course called "Modern Studies", and one day fishing

16

came up as a discussion, and Jim said that he liked it. The ensuing debate ended with Jim having to write a paper on the subject "What is good about fishing?"

To my knowledge, there has never been any systematic stocktaking of the arguments for angling. Dispersed throughout angling literature, the internet and angling journals, you'll find single strands and snippets of various arguments, which try to show the good of angling. The difficulty is, of course, that every angler intuitively knows, or thinks he knows, that angling is good. But that isn't really helpful if, for example, you have to make a case for angling (as opposed to defending it) and not on solely intuitive individual terms. Here is my own run-down of the most popular arguments, all of which have a grain of truth in them. I will provide a commentary on each as I go along. The listing and summarising of these arguments suggest a neatness that is misleading, because most of them overlap in one area or another.

Angling is a healthy outdoor pursuit

This seems so obviously to be the case. Angling can't be unhealthy, can it? But just what do "health" and "healthy" mean? The World Health Organisation (WHO) defines "health" as follows:

… a state of complete physical, mental and social well-being and not merely the absence of disease or infirmity.

Angling certainly is conducive to well-being because it has physical, mental and social components and can even help to regain competences in those fields. I have seen angling work at least temporary miracles with children afflicted with Attention Deficit Hyperactivity Disorder. Don't take "healthy" in the narrow sense like a particular activity like working out in the gym. Angling is healthy in a much wider sense: it caters for body and soul; and as for pure calorie burning, if you specialise in fishing mountain lakes, you can burn as many calories as you like.

Angling is relaxing

Strictly speaking, this is part of the health argument but as it is so important, it merits being listed under its own heading. Again, there is no doubt that angling is relaxing but what exactly does "relax" mean? The word is of Latin origin (*relaxare*) and means "to loosen" or "to open" and in this original sense describes best what happens. When you go fishing, you open up to different impressions and thoughts. Note that even if you completely loose your ties with the hustle and bustle of everyday life for a while, it is still you who are doing the fishing and not another person. You don't change personality when you go fishing. "To loosen" and "to open" is the precondition of successful angling in terms of catching fish and thinking about fishing and all that is linked to it. To be able "to loosen" and "to open" is a considerable achievement in itself.

Angling is a fascinating pastime

Again, intuitively, no doubt about it, but precision is needed here. Again the Latin origin of the word helps us understand. *Fascinare* means, "to bewitch" and in that sense describes the fact that the angler is completely taken in by angling and his whole attention is absorbed. "Fascinating" describes the fact that an object like a dapping fly dancing over the waves can transfix you so utterly that you forget that the rest of the world exists, and in such a condition time flies. This is why most of the time anglers turn up at home later than agreed.

Angling keeps the boys off the streets

And the girls, women and men, but for argument's sake let's stick to the boys. A boy hooked on fishing is not a likely candidate for getting into serious trouble. Why do I say "serious trouble"? All boys get into trouble of one kind or another. It's simply part of the process of growing up. Boys have to experience trouble and learn how to get out of it, which is the difficult bit. Drugs, fights over girls, quarrels with teachers or money-problems are trouble. They are "serious trouble" if you can't manage to get out of them. Somebody hooked on fishing has learned practical reasoning, how to approach and solve problems (you have to break the egg to make an omelette). Moreover somebody fishing probably has adult friends whom he might trust more than parents if he is in a jam. Young anglers in trouble usually get help. The poor non-anglers are at the mercy of the politically correct psychologists and social workers. Angling creates a mental and social climate in which positive problem solving is possible. Besides, angling literally keeps the boys off the street – they can't be in two places, i.e. the river and the streets, at the same time.

Angling satisfies a primitive need

This is probably the most popular argument stating that there is, in effect, a Neanderthal in each of us and that angling appeals to this remote ancestor. I have never met my Neanderthal and I am a bit suspicious of this evocation of a distant hunter-gatherer culture. Why? Doesn't it imply that for anglers the clock has stood still for hundreds of thousands of years while non-anglers live in the present and have evolved and discarded their Neanderthal? Wouldn't it be more accurate to say – in line with modern genetics – that angling as a disposition is simply part of the human being? Angling is primitive in the sense that it has always been and still is in our genes. Dispositions and talents are distributed unequally, which is why some people get hooked on fishing and others don't.

Angling is character-building

Winning is easy: anybody can win, there's really no achievement there; Losing and failing are difficult – you need character to keep up your spirits, not fall into despair but soldier on. Angling is not a game, and therefore you can't win: in angling you achieve. Catching a fish is an achievement and the road to achievement is often paved with failure, disasters and disappointment. Angling teaches you a great many things without your even noticing it.

Angling is fun

Where's the fun in getting soaked, gnawed at by midges and stung by nettles (to mention but a fraction of the minor and major obstacles between you and a fish)? Indeed, you might ask, where is the fun? Fun is, of course, the most subjective part of angling. For our present purpose it is enough here simply to state that angling is fun, pure enjoyment.

21

Angling inspires an understanding of nature

This is another didactic argument for angling. It expresses the fact that if the angler wants to be successful, he needs to know about nature. He is forced willy-nilly to observe, to reason and to act accordingly. **Without a minimal understanding of nature's ways you can never be a good fisherman.** There is, in my view, much more to it than that. Angling, I believe, is the king of sports because it draws you deeper into the workings of nature than any other field sport. Communion with nature is probably the essence of angling.

My angling friend Bill is a die-hard sceptic and a practical man. He's highly suspicious of "fancy stuff". The first question he fired at me when I told him I was enquiring into the beauty of angling was typical: "Alex, what's the use of that?" I was taken aback by his blunt utilitarian attitude. To me it seemed obvious that an enquiry into the beauty of angling needed no such justification. But then, even space missions need justifications for what is essentially curiosity. One of the justifications of landing on the moon surely is Teflon-coated backing. Whatever the cost-benefit analysis of space missions, the knowledge generated by the challenge is considerable. Likewise, I hope that my expedition into the uncharted territory of angling beauty will yield some knowledge or at least insight. So enquiring into the beauty of angling is like many other things, done just for the sake of it. Beyond that, there are two other reasons why such an undertaking could be of interest. Firstly, I don't think it has ever been done before. Bill might immediately object that there are thousands of writers who have praised the beauty of angling. Yes, I would say, but their praise is of literary nature: Izaak Walton aside, philosophical approaches are thinly spread in angling literature. Secondly, by attempting to establish the positive arguments for angling, I may contribute in a small way to keeping angling firmly rooted in our culture. Making a positive case for angling means more than airing personal views and impressions. It means inquiring whether or not there are objective grounds for holding that angling is good. In order to do so, we need to overcome two major obstacles: pain and cruelty.

In my recent book *Hook, Line and Thinker* I have exposed the misanthropic philosophies of the anti-anglers and conclusively shown that angling is not cruel. Since the publication of *Hook, Line and Thinker*, a study by the Roslin Institute claiming that fish feel

23

pain hit the headlines worldwide. This study will be quoted and referred to as authoritative by anti-anglers. The following article which I wrote in response to those "new" findings sums up the fish-feel-pain issue and clears the path to new zones of angling theory.

Trout Trauma Puts Scientists on the Hook?

Early this year (2002) a study by Dr. James Rose, University of Wyoming, concluded that it is impossible for fish to feel pain since fish do not have the brain structure for the experience. Then, hardly half a year later, came the fanfare from Edinburgh: according to scientists from the Roslin Institute (remember Dolly, the first sheep clone?) and the University of Edinburgh, fish can feel pain. What are anglers to make of this confusing contradiction? Whom are we to believe and what are the consequences for the future?

The first thing that struck me was the timing. Hardly had the ink dried on Dr. Rose's study than the world's newspapers were full of headlines about fish feeling pain. For the anti-angling lobby there couldn't have been a more timely moment for an attack on angling (also right at the beginning of the season in the northern hemisphere). I have no evidence that the timing was anything other than coincidental, but I wouldn't be at all surprised if such evidence were to emerge. After all, the Medway report (1979) and the Utrecht study (1988) on which anglers rested their case so far, are a bit worn out and no longer carry much conviction.

At first glance punctuation and style of presentation aren't of major importance in scientific issues. Nevertheless there is a point worth noting. There have been several official press releases from the institutions involved in this new study. Interestingly enough the headlines differ: "Trout trauma puts anglers on the hook?" is one version and the other is without the question mark. In either case it's an excellent headline for selling a story – full marks to the PR-department. It wouldn't have gained half the attention with the original title of the study by Dr. Lynne U. Sneddon, Dr. Victoria Braithwaite and Dr. Michael J. Gentle:

'Do fish have nociceptors: evidence for the evolution of a vertebrate sensory system'.

Question marks are, however, not the only knotty points in a study which is hailed as a shining example of clarity proving "hook, line and sinker that fish feel pain."

As the title indicates the study is about nociceptors. Nociceptors are receptor cells for noxious stimuli and the job of these cells is nociception i.e. detecting noxious stimuli. The authors claim that "relatively little attention has been paid to nociception" and "to date, little attention has been paid to potential pain perception in fish." Now that leaves me absolutely flabbergasted considering that it was exactly the point of Dr. Rose's work to scrutinise the relation between nociception and pain – and there is no doubt that nociception does not equal pain. In fact Dr. Rose's work isn't mentioned at all, as if it didn't exist! Is this a deliberate insult and an attempt to hush up his findings lest anglers get to know them? And "relatively little" in the academic world usually means there are already hundreds if not thousands of dissertations on that particular or related topics: nociception is not terra incognita! Why pretend otherwise?

The reason why Dr. Rose's work isn't even mentioned in the new study is because the authors would have had to be explicit about neurophysiological aspects and their assumptions about awareness in fish. Skipping the central issue of awareness and replacing it with vague assumptions and hints, the findings of Dr. Sneddon and her team in no way justify their conclusions – which is putting it politely.

The study is full of sloppy remarks like: "The polymodal nociceptors found here in the trout have similar properties to those found in amphibians, birds, and mammals including humans." Aha, I always thought there was a little trout in me. This similarity between trout and man was worked out long ago by folk wisdom: hence the expression "green around the gills". But seriously, what do "similar properties" mean? How much horse is in a man whose laugh is similar to neighing?

So far so good, but where the trout trauma is definitely thrown off the rails and getting itself into a hopeless tangle is in the discussion of human pain and animal pain. Human pain, so it is acknowledged, has an emotional dimension and requires awareness. Of animal emotion (awareness?) the authors say: "It is impossible to truly know if an animal has an emotion since we cannot measure emotion directly … what an animal 'feels' is possibly nothing like the experience of humans with a more complex brain structure. However the animal's experience may be unpleasant or cause suffering and its discomfort is no less important in terms of biology or ethics." These last few words could be straight from Tom Regan, Peter Singer or other "animal rights" philosophers.

Besides that, what can one make of it? Doesn't "it is impossible to truly know" mean "we can't know" and if so why not say so? Can emotion be measured indirectly? And think about this: they clearly state that human experience and trout experience are not the same. Yet they should be assumed to be the same and taken as the basis for ethical considerations: all trout are cute little humans with scales and fins. Again, a crystal-clear distinction is drawn between animal experience and human experience; but in the same breath (a few lines further) the authors conclude: "If a noxious event has sufficiently adverse effects on behaviour and physiology in an animal and this experience is painful in humans, then it is likely to be painful in the animal." I think this is a confused and incoherent statement.

The hard facts of the experiments conducted are not for the faint-hearted: injecting acetic acid and bee venom in the lips of one group of trout and sucking the brains out of the other (under anaesthetic). So the latter group isn't of interest to the fisherman because the fish he catches aren't brain-amputated. Of the former group it is said that the injections resulted in anomalous behaviour whereas a control group that had been injected saline behaved normally. The anomalous behaviour was "rubbing the injured area" and "rocking behaviour ... reminiscent of the stereotypal rocking behaviour of primates that is believed to be an indicator of poor welfare" ("reminiscent" like "similar" is a suggestive term – and what a bold leap from fish to primates).

Alright, but how does this anomalous behaviour prove that fish feel or experience pain and, in this particular case, are outraged (emotion) at the injustice of being experimented on? If I shoo away a wasp, does the wasp "understand" the implicit threat in my gestures and does it maybe "feel" rejected? If after rain the worms are out and I accidentally step on one it surely reacts but that reaction doesn't constitute an experience in the human sense. Reactions and responses of animals don't per se signify awareness or experience! That injection of a massive dose of bee venom and the trout's speedy recovery from it does not show that fish feel pain but rather that they are practically insensitive, which is consistent with the angler's observation of the same fish being caught twice or three times in succession. It also confirms another point commonly made by anglers: if the fish felt pain when hooked then it wouldn't run but would swim towards the angler.

Perhaps more enlightening than their study as such is the guideline they go by: "Assessing the subjective experiences of animals plays an increasingly large role in animal welfare" and in this they refer to authors like Broom and Dawkins (both committed to animal rights). Dr. Sneddon's team are not just an inch away from the tenets of animal rights – they're right in the centre of the animal rights camp.

The last sentence of the study encapsulates the style, spirit and content of the study perfectly: "Future work should examine the cognitive aspects of noxious stimulation to assess how important enduring a noxious, potentially painful event is to the mental well-being of this species." In other words now that they believe (they don't know) that fish feel pain they're going to torture and mutilate thousands of trout to find out just how badly it affects their psyche. That's very strange, to say the least, coming from a team which decided to limit their experiments with venom to six rainbow trout for "ethical reasons".

Talking of ethics and tactics: Dr. Sneddon is reported to have said that she had no problem with anyone who caught and quickly killed a fish for eating. Now anglers beware! Catch-and-release anglers of all kinds are implicated, which leaves the catch-and- eat anglers still in favour. Not for long though because "quickly" is a flexible term and will eventually be construed as "the fastest possible", which obliges again all anglers to fish with broomsticks and abseiling ropes. So long-term, all fishermen are going out of business on the basis of ethics. Whichever way you look at it, ethics is the central theme in all this.

The ostensible aim of the research was to examine nociceptors as "evidence for the evolution of a vertebrate sensory system". I am not an expert on the matter but some evidence might have been found and this might throw new light on some aspect in evolution. Most of the study is, however, quite simply focused on the question of pain in fish. The frequent inroads into related subjects like animal welfare, ethics or psychology and the way the study was handled on the PR side generates more than a little suspicion about the purpose of the study.

Conclusion: once more anglers are faced with wild anthropomorphic (attribution of human characteristics to non-human beings) speculation and accusations based on largely incomplete, muddled, half-baked, animal rights-tainted, highly speculative research. This new study is in no way a challenge to the work of Dr. James Rose, yet for years to come, anti-anglers and animal rightists will cite it as a conclusive. Be prepared! The research might have found new nociceptors but essentially the number of nociceptors doesn't say anything at all about what happens with the information in the fish brain. There, the matter of pain is decided and, fish, says British fish scientist Dr. Bruno Broughton, "literally don't have the brains for it".

The philosophical approach to the right to fish in *Hook, Line and Thinker* was in many ways defensive, dictated by circumstances. By the same token, many unpleasant things about anti-angling had to be discussed there. As the subtitle *Reflections on the Beauty of Angling* indicates, the focus in my present inquiry has shifted. It turns its back on the antis and their distorted, dangerous and revolting philosophies. They are, nevertheless, a fact of angling life. Centre stage will, now, be taken by the beauty of angling itself.

And that's the reason why we shall head straight back to *The Lobster* now. My most beautiful fish was the salmon we caught on Lough Currane on January 22, 2003. That salmon was the first of the season and the first one caught on the fly that year in Ireland. **"We" were Michael O' Sullivan and I.** Especially on Lough Currane it is the knowledge and skill of the ghillie that catches fish, no doubt about it. When Michael gets a call on his mobile from one of his fellow ghillies to inform him that a salmon has been caught, he relates the news to me as follows "Vincent (Dominic, Tom etc.) has caught a fish". Michael never says, for example "Robert (Vincent's client) has caught a fish". If on the contrary a fish gets away, Michael will describe the situation as "Robert lost a fish" or, in a milder mood, "They have lost a fish". Should we be the lucky boat to report a success, Michael will choose the plural: "We caught a fish." "Alex has lost a fish" hasn't happened yet (touch wood). This choice of words couldn't be less whimsical: it expresses the facts (A.A. Luce describes similar usage in *Fishing and Thinking*).

29

"There is no kelt in him," Michael judged after we had landed the fish and then wielded the priest. This done, he rang *The Lobster* and his colleagues to check whether ours was the first salmon. It was: nobody else had caught a fish, it was a perfect beauty and Michael and I were as happy as can be. There was another salmon on display that evening, the first one caught in the river Fertha. It was about the same size as ours, and the angler was tickled pink. Who wouldn't be? The Guinness pump in *The Lobster* ached under the strain, and everybody was in the best of spirits.

Next morning when I went to buy my sandwiches for lunch, the girl at the counter enquired, "Aren't you the man who caught the first salmon?" I proudly affirmed that I was and did the same a couple of minutes later at the petrol station. In a country where the angler is a well-liked figure and where fishing is held in proper esteem, important news travels fast. Michael was, understandably, in a cheerful mood, and as the boat headed out for new adventures, he told me the tidings of the previous night. I had left *The Lobster* shortly before my blood started to turn black. Michael, the other ghillies a few locals and a man from the Fishery Board, stayed on. When finally only an upright few were still there paying their respects to those salmon, Vincent loudly and clearly asserted: "That's a kelt!" pointing his finger at the salmon from the river Fertha.

Had anybody else dared such a challenge, there would have probably been a minor uproar but coming from Vincent this was different. Vincent rarely gets fishing matters wrong and consequently the half-dozen men all went over to the silver plates to inspect the salmon in question. It was examined and sure enough it turned out to be a kelt. Now that was sensational: of all the experienced ghillies and anglers, only one had spotted the fact. I remembered looking at the other salmon and thinking that it was not as beautiful as ours: it was not as "deep". I hadn't given that thought a chance to evolve but even if I had, I probably would have never guessed the truth. But there it was – a kelt – and Vincent, when asked how he could tell, said he simply had a feeling about that fish: "There's something wrong with him" were his words. But more than that, he had an explanation why that fish passed as a salmon with everybody. According to Vincent, the salmon of the Fertha just nip in to spawn and without further delay return to the sea. That being the case, the

30

salmon simply can't be bothered to change to kelts, i.e. to look like kelts. Vincent added emphatically that the angler can't be blamed for taking that fish. To drive the point home, he said that on the spot he would have taken it as well.

Having related all the news, after a short pause Michael said, "I would have never guessed it was a kelt." Then he fell silent. After a while he asserted with authority, "And I tell you another thing, Alex: that fish should never have been there in the first place," to which I duly rose with an amazed "Why?" "Well, the season on the Fertha doesn't open until February 1." Nobody had noticed that.

We spend most of our lives overlooking things. Someone has asked you, Jim, what is good about angling. This is a deceptively easy question. Ask ten anglers "What is good about angling?" and you'll see ten out of ten anglers confidently drawing in breath and poising themselves to answer immediately. To anglers, the answer to "What is good about angling?" seems as obvious as the answer to "What day is it today?" Everybody feels they know the answer. But conveying it is the hard part. Most anglers will spontaneously say "It's great", "I like it" or some such statement of approval, experience and pleasure. If individual approval, experience and pleasure were the answer, then there would be as many answers as there are fishermen. "As many answers as there are fishermen" is in turn equivalent to saying that there is no answer at all because all answers are tied to individual experience. There is no one answer. Supposing that to be the case, individuals might share and understand (to a degree) overlapping experiences, but we couldn't possibly agree on the answer to "What is good about angling?" because by definition that answer is tied to the individual. Your answer is as good as mine.

Is it really? All angling stories circle around the same theme: man tries to catch fish with hook, line and rod. Underlying that activity are a million and one individual motives, desires, reasons and techniques, but all anglers aim to catch fish, which is more than a mere similarity in appearance: all anglers recognise that it is good to go fishing, i.e. to try and catch fish. It would be unreasonable for an angler to say it is not good to catch fish. Common sense and reason tell us that every action and pursuit aims "at the good". The meaning of aiming at the good is straightforward: a programmer wants to write good programs so he can sell them; a footballer wants to play good football so that his team wins; and an angler wants to go out and do some good fishing, i.e. to catch fish. The elementary sense of "good" in angling is to go out and try to catch fish but as all anglers know and all angling writers over the centuries have pointed out, there is more to fishing than catching fish.

That "more" is a fact. The "more" of fishing is, however, beyond raw experience. It's a bit like the most elusive of all facts: "love". Anybody who has ever fallen in love will testify that love exists but what exactly it is, people, poets and philosophers find hard to say. Literally thousands of angling writers have tried their hand at that "more" and there are, hopefully, thousands to follow, because as long as anglers mull over fishing, angling will live. Angling literature seems like individualism pure and simple; no writing angler holds back personal experiences or his views. In fact, there is probably no genre as chatty as angling literature. Nevertheless, angling literature is thriving, because readers of angling books are acquainted with and love the basic plot of all angling literature: man goes fishing with rod, line and hook – it's as simple as the other basic plot to which everybody can relate: boy meets girl or the other way round.

In his *Haunted by Waters*, Mark Browning analyses fly fishing in North American angling literature and at one point contrasts the British school with the American tradition. The former he characterises by the use of "the reductive logic of Descartes", while "North American writers would be more apt to use thought patterns drawn from Lao Tzu". Now that's an interesting juxtaposition. "I think, therefore I am" is probably the best-known dictum of the French philosopher and mathematician René Descartes (1596–1650). The hallmarks of Cartesian philosophy are its rationality, logic and clarity.

"Stop thinking, and end your problems" is ascribed to Lao Tzu (c. 600 B.C.), as is the famous Tao Te Ching, in which he lays the foundations of Taoism. Taoism is a philosophy aiming at simplicity, freedom of desire and eventually a withdrawal from the world by giving up all striving. The meaning of "reductive logic" seems clear enough. "Thought patterns", in contrast, bubble with ambiguity and I find it difficult to swallow that American angling writers should rely on "thought patterns" implying that they shouldn't go fishing in the first place (trying to catch a trout is striving for something). "Reductive logic" suggests a sort of binding certitude while "thought patterns" are strangely non-committal. As there are a thousand and one versions of Taoism and Lao Tzu texts, it is likely that one of them is compatible with going fishing and that's the one Browning had in mind. But whatever the case, in all the thousands of angling books on either side of the Atlantic and elsewhere you'll find with dead certainty, in one form or another, a reference to that "more" – the very fact that somebody feels compelled to write an angling book proves that there is more to fishing than catching fish. There is unanimous agreement on the fact that there is that "more", but the moment you try to put your finger on it, it's gone. The main point I want to make here, though, concerns not interpretations of the history of angling literature but rather the universal fact that this "more" unites all anglers. It is universally experienced and acknowledged, which means that it, like love, transcends mere individual experiences.

Let's look at the hook now: I have heard people say the hook is a nasty piece of work. Some people seem to be almost scared of hooks, as if something evil dwells within them. The key to understanding this is empathy. Empathy is a wonderful human ability, and I suppose many people feel for the hooked fish and somehow imagine their own selves dangling from that hook. But what exactly does that mean? Could it be that people disturbed by the alleged cruelty of angling are just trying to protect themselves, that the intensity of the emotions they display conceals their dread of a fish being caught on a hook? They are not interested in the fish but in themselves. They suffer from hookophobia, the sole cure to which is a ban on angling because only then can they be sure that no fish will be caught with a hook. Anti-angling and , by the same token, other "animal rights" propaganda has more to do with a certain group of people's mindset than with pain in fish and other animals. If the "suffering" of the fox were really the concern of the anti-hunters, why not ban cars – road traffic is the source of an infinite amount of "suffering" in the world of foxes. Be that as it may, some people express their feelings by saying something along the lines of "Fish don't enjoy being caught".

Those who do are kind and considerate but, to put it bluntly, they haven't thought the least bit about what they are saying. So what are they saying when they claim that fish "don't enjoy being caught"?

The essential import is, of course, that fish are capable of enjoying or not enjoying certain things such as being caught or not being caught. Now, that's a tall order for fish – just think of the million and one things we can enjoy, e.g. riding a bicycle, reading a book, reciting poetry or playing football. Fish are excluded because they simply can't do any of those things. The reason? Fish are fish and human beings are human beings. Fish can't enjoy what humans enjoy, and humans can't enjoy what fish enjoy. Oops – I have said it myself now: "fish enjoy" – but there is a vital difference in my usage. I am aware that I employ the term only because there is no other way than to apply certain human terms – we say that fish "fight" – but this in no way implies that the experience of the fish is the same as the human experience. If there is such a thing as fish joy, we'll never be able to know what that is. What we do know for certain is that the fish brain is not a miniature human brain and that its structure is radically different to that of the human brain. The nature of the fish brain makes it impossible for fish to feel pain as we know it, or "joy". A fish can't "enjoy" not being caught. Footloose and fancy-free swimming about is not in the repertoire of fish. Nor are pain and suffering. Of course, the sensorium of the fish includes nociceptors, i.e. receptor cells capable of detecting noxious stimuli. But nociception, which triggers off reactions is, as we have seen, quite different from feeling pain. Nociception does not equal pain. Fish don't feel pain – nor, by the same token, pleasure.

Now imagine a caveman sitting on the bank of a river idly watching some fish leaping about. Then, like a bolt from the blue, inspiration strikes: before his mind's eye he sees the hook and immediately realises that he has invented the fishing hook. Nonsense. Neither that caveman nor any other man "invented" the fishing hook. **The fishing hook was discovered. It was there all the time,** so to speak, and for that discovery to be made, completely different entities had to be combined. First, the hook itself: a suitably shaped piece of wood or bone. The potential of the object would have had to be recognised in such a way as to form the idea of attaching it to a line. Then comes the line: like the spear, it greatly increased the range of the arm and opened up new areas in which human beings could fish. Later on the rod would point the way to new piscatorial possibilities. All this presupposed the mastering of techniques to produce line which stood up to the task.

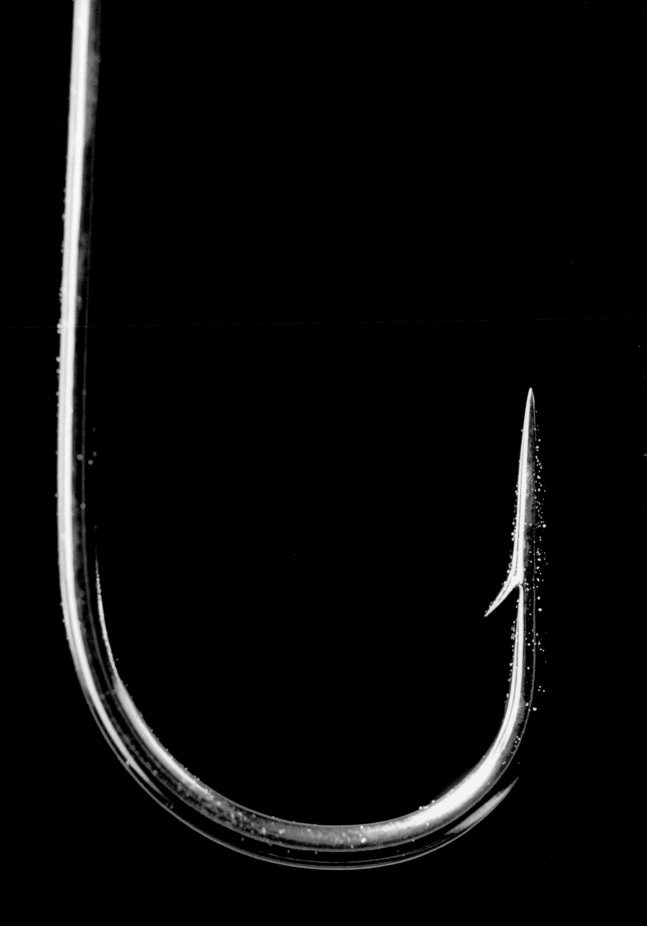

But hook and line by themselves were not sufficient to fish with – they had to be joined by that most intriguing achievement of mankind: the knot.

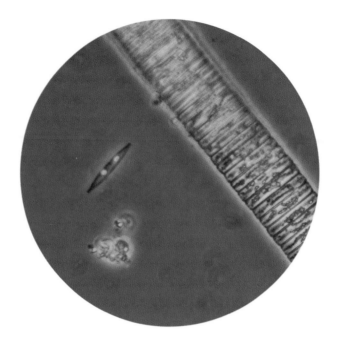

30,000 to 40,000 years ago, survival entailed unbelievable hardships. Hunting, fishing and gathering whatever was deemed edible was the key to life for thousands and thousands of years. Later on a pastoral economy and agriculture in the modern sense changed production. Hunting and gathering, though still part of life, in due course lost their prime importance in the Western world. Fishing, by contrast, remains to this very day an important economic factor in many countries. Yet in order to keep things in proportion we should remember that only recently (around 1960) has it been possible to rely on a constant food supply. Food security in the Western world is a great success story rarely appreciated in its full amplitude today. Our grandmothers and grandfathers still knew scarcity, and saying grace had a real meaning, which was lost in the intervening years. These days you're more likely to pray for protection from food ingredients of doubtful origin.

Houses have replaced caves, and maybe today's job market is yesterday's hunting grounds. With food security, health services, computers, mobility, entertainment and all the amenities of the contemporary world we are, materially speaking, light-centuries away from caves and clubs. However, if you look at it closely, the line dividing us from cavemen is a thin one. On the clock of earth history the Stone Age is but a tick away! The circumstances of life might have been different in the very, very distant past, but **what was human about humans then is still so today.** Reason, laughter, love, hope: the entire range of emotions, inclinations, talents and skills, then as now, define a clear border between man and animals. Among those inclinations and talents is fishing. Look into any culture at any time anywhere and you'll find that where there are fish there are fishermen trying to catch them. Fishing in whatever form is part of human culture, and in its history the hook was a major technological breakthrough. It is also an amazing fact that from the dawn of mankind up to the present day, the concept of the fishing hook hasn't changed. The fishing hook is truly one of the most fascinating and everlasting "inventions", and its beauty lies in its simplicity.

To many people, angling is simply second nature. Why should it have no place in the modern world, as some people argue? What can be wrong with an activity so much in line with nature and conservation? The father of the modern concept of conservation, by the way, was none other than the famous American angler Gifford Pinchot. Fishing isn't cruel – anyone proclaiming otherwise is being polemical, probably in order to launch an attack on angling. Serious anti-angling is not based so much on compassion for the "poor fish" but what are generally called "animal rights". Peter Singer, who is widely acclaimed as the father of animal rights, paradoxically enough does not believe in rights. His hobbyhorse is "animal liberation". Animals should be liberated from human exploitation (e.g. riding horses) and the species barrier should fall. Tom Regan is the most famous advocate of animal rights. In his system the species barrier also crumbles, but in contrast to Singer his animals aren't simply liberated; they are granted rights. The most basic one of these is the right to life. In accordance with general usage I employ "animal rights" to cover both concepts.

Imagine this most basic of rights in practice: I swat a fly. Another fly (with the right to life) witnesses this murder and is duty-bound to report it. Can the witness fly alert the police? Or will the bird that sat on a branch just outside the window raise the alarm? Hardly: it gulped an insect a minute ago and is not going to rat on me. Animal liberation and animal rights are philosophies condemning angling but Peter Singer, for example, condones killing perfectly healthy babies and thinks bestiality could be great fun and that there is nothing wrong with it. All their talk about sentience, rights and compassion is mere beating about the bush. What animal rights is all about is the uprooting of all traditional Western values. There is a dangerous egalitarianism at work here and a renaissance of totalitarian thinking. **How can man not be special – do you know of another "animal" that goes fishing with hook and line?** Human beings are the pinnacle of God's Creation. And even if you wish to leave God out of it, you can't ignore the facts staring you in the face: man's position among all living beings is unique. Disregarding this, as some animal rightists persistently and systematically do, is tantamount to misanthropy and inhumanity.

The basic "design" of the hook hasn't changed in aeons because it can't be improved. The hook is one of the few objects with a definitive shape. Of course, the experts will point out that there are different styles of modern hooks – such as the Aberdeen, the Perfect or the Wilson – but these are technical aspects which don't have any bearing whatsoever on the hook as such. Anglers have become so used to the hook that we seldom appreciate it in the same way as, say, a fishing rod. When you're in the tackle shop, the rods arrayed on the racks immediately attract your attention. You pick one up, you touch it, you feel its balance, you admire the craftsmanship, and before you know it, your mind begins to wander: the river, the lake, the fish…

The rod has an immediate impact on the fisherman's imagination, whereas the hook and the line are clearly the wallflowers in the tackle shop and in the fisherman's mind. In comparison with the rod or reel they're somehow nondescript entities simply taken for granted. Or take the float displays: if you look at a float, you start fishing immediately – you can't help it! The same doesn't happen with the hook or the line. Is it perhaps because the hook and the line have become part of the fisherman himself? The fisherman's brain no longer classifies them as objects any more but as an organic part of himself. As such hook and line don't excite the fisherman in the same way as do the external objects such as rod, reel or float.

Let's nevertheless have a look at the hook as an object. Hooks are abundant. This wasn't always the case: they used to be individual objects (like the line) crafted with great care and well looked after. The skill, material, time and energy needed to produce hooks made them valuable objects. As long as they were hard to come by and expensive, they perhaps caught the imagination of the fisherman. I don't believe that though, because price is never the whole story: floats, for example, don't cost the world, either. Contemporary hooks are easily produced and very refined objects in terms of material- and quality. Their very abundance hides the fact that a hook is a superb object. If you look at a well-manufactured modern hook closely, you'll discover a high-tech product with a first-class finish in terms of precision and smoothness, which together with its simplicity and non-improvable functionality make it an aesthetically pleasing object.

The hook is not a tool like a hammer or a knife. It's not a weapon, either; it's an object which is of no use on its own. Only the line and the knot and the fisherman can make it work. The hook (and the bait), the line, the knot and the fisherman are completely interdependent. Take one element out of it and the whole concept is no longer viable. Putting all this together 30,000 or 40,000 years ago (or even earlier) was some feat. Catching fish with hook and line has a pedigree like no other human endeavour has. All human societies sooner or later discovered the hook for fishing, and in all worlds fishing has been regarded as a good. Tradition interpreted in the sense that fishing always has been and always will be a good for man is as sound an argument for angling as any. Before continuing to follow the track of the hook, I have to digress a little in order to clarify the usage of "tradition". This is a word that comes into play whenever there is a discussion on the more fundamental aspects of hunting, fishing and country life. Many people use the word in many ways. In order to reduce misunderstandings to a minimum, let me explain what I see as tradition.

THE GIANT
NOBLEMAN

Is it not the case, you might ask, that "tradition" and "traditional values" simply reflect a defensive attitude, a smokescreen because many anglers, understandably, don't want to be bothered with anti-fishing, anti-hunting or anti-countryside attitudes? I don't think so. The recourse to tradition and traditional values goes way beyond a merely defensive reflex to shoo off disagreeable ideas. What is quintessentially meant by "tradition" is not some folklore of cloudy origin, not some special 300-year-old fishing technique or code. "Tradition" stands first and foremost for Christianity and its culture. This is why "tradition" raises the hackle of many urban intellectuals. Modern thought is basically materialistic, atheistic and relativistic and wants to do away with Christianity and its values, knowledge and wisdom. The reason for that is that to the nice urban intellectuals, Christianity is the main obstacle to achieving a modern world, one that is cruelty-free and where, long-term, vegetarianism is enforced by law. These modern philosophies and their political support are, as in anti-hunting and anti-fishing, neo-totalitarian: communism and fascism celebrate a comeback in the guise of animal rights and compassion. When I said above that "tradition interpreted in the sense that fishing always has been and always will be a good for man", I meant that Christian tradition especially has seen it as good (actually all traditions see it as good), and before that it couldn't have been seen as anything other than good. Izaak Walton remarks:

I shall content myself in telling you, that angling is much more ancient than the Incarnation of our Saviour; for in the prophet Amos mention is made of fish-hooks; and in the book of Job (which was long before the days of Amos, for that book is said to be writ by Moses) mention is made also of fish-hooks, which must imply anglers in those times.

He is then quick to point out a couple of pages later:

And for the lawfulness of fishing: it may very well be maintained by our Saviour's bidding St Peter cast his hook into the water and catch a fish, for money to pay tribute to Caesar.

Traditional moral values have had a hard time during the past 40 years or so: they are ridiculed by an alliance of philosophers, atheists and well-meaning social reformers, all working in one way or another to destroy the Christian mores. The reason is that these people see the tenets of Christianity as stifling progress. What exactly do I mean by "traditional moral values", you rightly ask? Common to Christendom are the Ten Commandments. These are the fundamentals of Christian ethics; by and large they form the basis of most people's ethical life. While some of the Commandments seem to have lost touch with present-day reality, others are undisputed. There is no need here to go into detail; the main thing is the broad consensus about those Ten Commandments. Although many people, including myself, don't even know what they are verbatim, we act by that general credence. It is that body of general moral guidelines and thought that I mean when I talk of "traditional moral values".

The years of incessant Christianity-bashing in regard to "tradition" and "traditional moral values" have created a spiritual uncertainty and a vacuum. This has been filled by esotericism and other ersatz. This trend is encouraged by so-called progressive philosophies, whose "moral" systems are not able to cater for the practical and religious needs of people. **Modern philosophies tend to be soulless and godless.** The prominent animal rights (Tom Regan) and animal liberation (Peter Singer) philosophies are materialistic and atheistic to the core. They reduce the human being to a mouldable material mass (without the least regard for the soul). You can take soul here in any sense you want: it simply expresses the fact that there is more to human beings than 70% water and 30% solid material.

The reason why these modern philosophies are leaving nothing but havoc in their clinical trail is that they can't be bothered with human beings, the Western world or its tradition. In supreme self-confidence and arrogance bordering on plain stupidity, they declare the last couple of thousand years of culture as null and void. Tradition is anathema to them because they see in it the root of all evil. All they have to offer instead is "political correctness".

Anti-angling is, so to speak, a sideshow in a sustained and determined attack to dissolve Western values. My angling friend Bill finds this a bit far-fetched and doesn't think it has anything to do with angling. But look at it from the political side: animal rights, i.e. anti-angling, is part of that wider movement engulfed by political correctness. The political correctness palette features most prominently: race, class, gender, sexual orientation, environment, animal rights and multiculturalism. The place of what was the class struggle has been taken over by the battle for your mind. At the linguistic level this battle has been raging incessantly for decades, and to illustrate as well as to brighten up what is in fact a depressing subject, I quote here from a politically correct Christmas card (various internet sources):

Please accept with no obligation, implied or implicit, our best wishes for an environmentally conscious, socially responsible, low-stress, non-addictive, gender-neutral celebration of the winter solstice holiday, practiced within the most enjoyable traditions of the religious persuasion of your choice, or secular practices of your choice, with respect for the religious/secular persuasions and/or traditions of others, or their choice not to practice religious or secular traditions at all...

And a fiscally successful, personally fulfilling and medically uncomplicated recognition of the onset of the generally accepted calendar year 2004, but not without due respect for the calendars of choice of other cultures whose contributions to society have helped make America great (not to imply that America is necessarily greater than any other country or is the only "America" in the western hemisphere), and without regard to race, creed, color, age, physical ability, religious faith, choice of computer platform, or sexual preference of the wishee.

(By accepting this greeting, you are accepting these terms. This greeting is subject to clarification or withdrawal. It is freely transferable with no alteration to the original greeting. It implies no promise by the wisher to actually implement any of the wishes for her/himself or others, and is void where prohibited by law,

*and is revocable at the sole discretion of the wisher. This wish is warranted to
perform as expected within the usual application of good tidings for a period
of one year, or until the issuance of a subsequent holiday greeting, whichever
comes first, and warranty is limited to replacement of this wish or issuance of a
new wish at the sole discretion of the wisher.)*

I understand that in some American universities, there is
mandatory "sensitivity training" aimed at purging the freshman's
language of politically incorrect terms. Add to this "Prejudice
Reduction Committees" and the like, and you begin to understand
that political correctness aims at nothing less than total control over
mind and heart: you're no longer free to think and feel, let alone
talk, as an individual but you have to conform to the prescriptive
norms of political correctness. I am sure you grasp the monstrosity
of this: it means nothing less than you as an individual ceasing to
exist. Big Brother is thinking for you. The common denominator of
all these philosophies is their essentially anti-Christian and anti-
Western stand: they would like to see Western society gone today
rather than tomorrow. Multiculturalism is about doing away with
culture: take the culture away and what you have left is "multism".
What a future! The slogan "Hey, hey, ho, ho, Western culture's gotta
go" by the Rev. Jesse Jackson (http://www.apca.com/11122001.html)
sums up perfectly the mission of political correctness.

Now, before you – like Bill – throw up your hands in despair and
say, "But Alex, come on, where is fishing in all this?", consider the
implications of the fact that animal rights is part and parcel of the
political-correctness package and that these ideas are the staple diet
of students of philosophy (and sociology, psychology etc.) students
throughout the Western world. From the universities the opposition
to tradition permeates the educational system, and before you know
it, angling is on the agenda for abolition. It is of vital importance
that anglers recognise the source and arguments of anti-angling.
Still not convinced that philosophy is a decisive factor for saving
fieldsports? Then consider the prominent animal rights and anti-
field-sports philosopher Andrew Linzey. He doesn't just sit in an
ivory tower somewhere but together with the Prime Minister, in
the policy-shaping committee of the Labour Party (see for example
http://observer.guardian.co.uk/politics/story/0,6903,967929,00.
html). Make no mistake: if a ban on angling weren't political suicide,

it would be done today! Make no mistake about it. A little bit more about this later on.

Political correctness has many faces, but when the cards are laid on the table, there will always be Christianity-bashing, Western culture-demonising and general ridiculing of traditional values. On the "positive" side you'll invariably find elements of materialism, relativism, nihilism and related ideas and concepts. These isms, boring, bewildering and confusing as they may be, are, in combination with animal rights, the nails in the coffin of fieldsports. Here are the most important of these isms, which are all interrelated:

Materialism
Materialism is the view that matter is all that matters and the only reality. All is cause and effect in the physical, material world. There is no room for God or a soul in the materialist world.

Relativism
Relativism comes in many guises, but all relativism holds that values and truth can never be absolute. Cultural relativism holds that the standards of a culture or society determine what is true in that culture at a given time. There can be as many truths as there are societies. A cousin of relativism is subjectivism: only my personal opinion is true for me.

Nihilism
Nihilism is the view that there are no values at all. A nihilist believes in nothing and actively tries to destroy the social and political structures of society, since they stand in the way of freedom.

Egalitarianism
Egalitarianism is the belief that all people have equal rights in all things. Usually, not always, this means the end of private property, expropriation and redistribution.

Atheism
Atheism simply means believing there is no God

Back to tradition: the meaning of "tradition" lies in the Greek word *paradosis*, which meant the handing on of Divine Revelation. In the Roman world the word appeared as trado and acquired a range of meanings involving, among other ideas, those of handing on, entrusting, reporting and instructing. Tradition is a dynamic process that not only secures knowledge but also expands it. In the wide sense in which I use the word, it refers to Christian culture, and in a narrower sense tradition refers to customs and beliefs of how to go about things. You can find tradition in all aspects of life: in folklore, in fishing, in cooking, in dress, and in flytying. Traditions in the narrow sense are discoveries or inventions. The rules governing traditional dress, for example, had to be laid down at one point. A tradition does not simply exist like a mountain: behind every tradition there is a decision about rules and standards, which are then handed down from one generation to the next. If it's a successful tradition, that is: there are also traditions that simply ebb away.

Traditionally, the trout season here begins some time in March and comes to a close towards the end of September. Today there is a trend in Britain and the United States to all-year fishing in self-contained stocked waters. But even in "normal" rivers people are considering introducing all-year fishing with catch-and-release in what used to be the closed season. Suppose, just suppose, all year fishing for trout (and salmon) were introduced. What would happen then to all the traditional opening ceremonies celebrated all over the trout- and salmon-fishing world? Once they lose their *raison d'être* the celebrations surely become meaningless. It would be highly absurd to celebrate what used to be the opening day – wouldn't the people involved feel rather silly doing so? The closed season respects the rhythm of nature and gives you time to recover, reflect, repair and prepare. An all-year season in all waters would make a farce of the happy anticipation of the opening day. A tradition is also a common ground which creates bonds and obligations, however loose, between people. I think that **much of the bemoaned moral decay of European societies has to do with the piecemeal disappearance of all sorts of minor traditions,** because all traditions create values which are respected by those adhering to that particular tradition. Realising that there are values and respecting them in this sense is minimal moral education. All traditions of whatever kind cultivate the idea

that there are obligations between people. Withering traditions signal the steady erosion of ethos and precede disorientation. Now that sounds positively way over the top – an all-year season in some waters surely won't precipitate Europe into anarchy. Well, some people would say we're already there, others will laugh the very proposition off and my own opinion is that it's high time to react on the value issue in general. I personally dislike the idea of poking for trout in winter. Grayling, of course, is another matter.

Tradition is a source of stability and order. Stability and order are preconditions for creative development and progress, and conservatism aims at preserving a basic stability and order, i.e. the platform from which economic, cultural and fishing projects can take off. That is why many socialists and leftists are conservative at heart. They, too, want stability and order. The disagreement with the conservatives originates in contentiousness about the nature of that platform: who contributes what and how to construct it? However, the consensus about stability and order, i.e. tradition, still weighs stronger than the differences in opinion over how to go about things and how to deal with challenges for change. **Fishermen are regularly caught in conflicts between tradition and innovation, between old, trusted tools and techniques and new, unknown products and methods, between good old habits and new possibilities.**

It might sound silly to you, but I once suffered sleepless nights because of fishing rods. Although my first fishing rod was a bamboo pole, I grew up with fibreglass rods. The Sixties were the age of fibreglass, which replaced cane. So, since I hadn't been acquainted with cane rods, there was never any question of conflict in terms of material. In my fly-fishing career I graduated from Shakespeare to Bruce & Walker and from there, dream of dreams, to Hardy. Where, then, do the sleepless nights come in? Years back I made one of my regular pilgrimages to the tackle shop. There, the tackle dealer unleashed his entire power of persuasion on me to try one of those rods he had just got in from America. "Sage," he said with a meaningful air as if that would explain something. To cut a long story short, he didn't get me to try the Sage that day but next time round I gave in. Trying that rod sent me through a variety of moods

ranging from disbelief to utter amazement: the balance, power and control were out of this world. The Sage reduced everything else to broomsticks. Yet my sentimental attachment to Hardy wasn't easily overcome. The source of that attachment was all the beautiful fishing I had done with my Hardy rods over the years and my belief in the brand. My Hardys were more than objects: they were companions, and parting with them seemed an awful prospect and a terrible thing to do, so I decided to postpone the decision and think it over. I was, of course, deceiving myself: the decision was already made, and in the nights that followed I was merely reliving my life with the Hardy rods. Then on a Saturday I bought my first Sage and have never looked back since.

Sometimes I think the nature of angling consists of dilemmas and contradictions. It is surely one of life's most doubt-generating pastimes. Laurence Catlow, in his fascinating and inspiring *Once a Flyfisher*, certainly knows the delicate and intricate aspects of angling conflicts well: the situation is that he has bought a few Klinkhamer flies on impulse and is now about to use one:

A strange sort of fear now came over me: lest the Klinkhamer would go on to catch me trout after trout, finally convincing me of the progressive nature of the fisher's and the fly dresser's art, finally persuading me that all my Orange Partridges and August Blacks and Waterhen Bloas had, along with all their cousins of the great spider clan, been shamed and superseded by modern flies, flies with gaudy tails of gold or with bent shanks and parachute wings and with foreign and repulsive names. It seemed that with my American rod of carbon fibre and with my fly from Holland, I had at last betrayed the long tradition of a Yorkshire trout stream. I wondered what Pritt's ghost would think of me and wondered if I should parade my contempt for his outmoded ways by getting myself one of those fishing waistcoats with a thousand pockets to fill with at least a thousand articles of essential gear. My lack of a pair of polarised glasses seemed suddenly reprehensible, and I felt a sudden longing for one of those wooden framed landing nets: the sort that hangs down your back and is so small that a gudgeon would have to try very hard to squeeze into it. I thought I might as well go the whole hog and buy a baseball cap to adorn my head on fishing days. Very few modern fishers are without one.

These few lines capture aptly and in quietly smiling fashion the tortuous exercise of trying to harmonise tradition and innovation on the level of tackle and equipment. Note that the author doesn't mention the reel, the fly line or the monofilament at all and just mentions the hook *en passant*. Yet the monofilament and the fly line, i.e. the improvements in that department during the author's fishing life, were truly revolutionary. It would seem that this passage bears out what I mentioned earlier, i.e. that the line is an integral part of the fisherman. Purity in tradition regarding equipment is impossible and, I think, undesirable as well. What would be the point of fishing with a greenheart rod, horsehair and leaking footwear today? What equipment-wise was right and useful in the past needn't be right and useful today; what was revolutionary yesterday is traditional today. In fact, our famous fishing forebears were wont to innovate and look for novel approaches aimed at improving their effectiveness. Isn't it precisely a quality of the good angler to look at things openly and inquisitively with an eye to improvement?

Having said that, I nevertheless share Laurence Catlow's attitude of doubt and hesitation, which runs deeper than a mere dislike of gaudy fly tails and modern materials. The key to piscatorial harmony in this respect is knowing when to throw caution and conventional wisdom to the wind. A couple of weeks back in July, my dear fishing friend Roland from Belgium visited us here in Switzerland for the weekend. Although I had assured him that he needn't bother bringing along his fishing gear, he did. The plan was that I would introduce him to fishing whitefish the traditional way. On our way to Lake Thun, Roland, a passionate fly fisherman, inquired about the possibilities of fly-fishing for the whitefish and about fly fishing on Lake Thun in general. I described my past efforts which hadn't yielded much to write home about. I had tried for whitefish, pike, perch and lake trout. The latter, I had concluded, were impossible to catch on the fly because at the depths they cruise at most of the time, they can't be reached. With the whitefish the problem is different: although they do take surface food, they are not regular, predictable risers like trout, and their take is untidy and splashy. As I meandered on with the description of my various experiments, techniques and flies, I hit on the topic of mayflies and heard myself saying, "I can't for the life of me imagine that these massive hatches of mayfly don't somehow play into the whitefish and trout diet." The moment

I said that, I realised that all these years I must have missed some golden opportunities. Mayfly hatches on Lake Thun are occasionally on such a scale that besides the swallows, which have a regular interest, seagulls, coots and swans join in the feast. Lake Thun's mayflies are king size, juicy and shine with an intensity of colour which almost seems to cry, "Eat me!" to the swallows. Besides being of great piscatorial importance, mayflies are the prima ballerinas of the freshwater universe. The unobtrusive and ethereal beauty of the mayfly hatch, nothing short of a miracle, has been immortalised by America's poet laureate Richard Wilbur:

Mayflies

In somber forest, when the sun was low,
I saw from unseen pools a mist of flies
In their quadrillions rise
And animate a ragged patch of glow
With sudden glittering – as when a crowd
Of stars appear
Through a brief gap in black and driven cloud,
One arc of their great round-dance showing clear.

It was no muddled swarm I witnessed, for
In entrechats each fluttering insect there
Rose two steep yards in air,
Then slowly floated down to climb once more,
So that they all composed a manifold
And figured scene,
And seemed the weavers of some cloth of gold,
Or the fine pistons of some bright machine.

Watching those lifelong dancers of a day
As night closed in, I felt myself alone
In a life too much my own,
More mortal in my separateness than they –
Unless, I thought, I had been called to be
Not fly or star
But one whose task is joyfully to see
How fair the fiats of the caller are.

Beautiful isn't it? (Richard Wilbur, *Mayflies*, Harcourt, Inc., New York, 2000. Quoted with kind permission of the publishers).

As it happened, there was towards the evening of that day a small mayfly hatch, but the stunner of that day, for me, was Roland catching whitefish not by the traditional method but with a fly. The secret weapon was bung and buzzer. While I too had tried buzzers, I had never fished them with the bung (I don't read angling magazines often – maybe I should – so the idea was new to me). The bung is not a fly but a piece of foam and a loop of monofilament tied to a hook. The set-up of the long cast is simple: at the tail it's a gold bead nymph acting as bait and weight; then come two buzzers and the bob, which is the bung or the bung-float because the bung is a float disguised as a fly. Anyway, with this contraption Roland caught whitefish on the fly – which I had never succeeded in doing. I was gobsmacked. Roland's unbiased approach reopened my eyes to the possibilities of fly-fishing on Lake Thun. The week following Roland's visit saw two significant mayfly hatches. My renewed interest and the bung (mayfly emerger on bung) resulted in my first trout catch on the fly on Lake Thun. Had I not received the outside impulse and been open-minded about it, I probably would never have taken up fly-fishing on Lake Thun again.

Although tradition can manifest itself visually, for example, in equipment, flies, techniques or dress, the essence of tradition is knowledge, which needs, no specific form or appearance. Having said that, I think in the application of it, certain standards are highly desirable and easier to keep if you're rooted to them. Take dress. How does dress come into fishing and its beauty? When I was a boy and a young man, the meadows were my safe haven. Dress, apart from its utility, was not a consideration either for me or anybody else. Given that fishing now and then involves smells, dirt and shredded trousers, only the cheapest or oldest was worn for fishing. This rag fashion was not a style born out of poverty: even the guys with the "big permit" (more of which later) went fishing in thinly disguised rags. The only distinguishing mark of the better-off anglers was sometimes a green sports jacket and a hat. I didn't see the significance and implication of all that back then, but I see it clearly now: fishing, according to the message of the general dress style, is a dirty, rough-tough business. I think in many instances dress reflects an attitude. Unless there are special circumstances, you don't go to a funeral in the brightest of dresses and you switch off your mobile phone, which these days is part of dress. Or, again, as a rule, you don't go half naked into a supermarket as many people do while on holiday in southern countries. Now this has nothing to do with etiquette or the notion that "clothes make the man". No, it has to do more with your attitude, i.e. how you regard what you do, how you regard others and dress is also a measure of your self-esteem.

Roland, who was a professional guide in the tropics, told me a story which touches on dress and more. One day he received a booking from a well-known industrialist, jet-setter and nobleman: the Duc de X. The man described himself on the phone as an angler and said he would like to fish with the fly for sailfish. At eight o'clock on the agreed day, the fishing yacht, captain, crew and Roland were ready. Conditions were ideal and everybody was eager to cast off. There was, however, no Duc in sight. Around nine o'clock, five people – instead of the two booked – appeared on the beach. One of the boat boys was already at the beach and transferred the three women in the party to the yacht. All scantily clad as if for a certain type of glamour photo. The two men waited on the beach, and one of them – with a gargantuan weight problem emphasised by the silly flower shorts he was wearing – grew impatient. He strode into the water and started swimming for the yacht, which was anchored maybe 200 yards from the shore. Now that doesn't seem much, but to swim 200 yards against the current can be a colossal effort. Panting and swearing (at what nobody knew) the Duc was heaved on board. The boat boy had in the meantime fetched the other man, who turned out to be the secretary, whom the Duc after regaining his breath, bawled at to get him so-and-so on the mobile and on the double. The captain too was shouted at when he started the engine: couldn't he wait until the Duc had finished his call? Call finished, the captain re-started the engines and off they went, only to stop after twenty minutes because guess who needed to make yet another call (a pattern which was repeated all day). Roland had noticed that the Duc had not protected himself with sunblock and offered him the bottle, only to get a surly "non!" Things went from bad to worse. The wind had picked up a bit, enough to make two of the ladies seasick. Presumably, it was the champagne the night before taking its toll.

Whatever, proportional to the intensity of the ladies' sickness, the Duc's humour brightened. He mercilessly poked fun at them and enjoyed himself. The captain and Roland, however, were worried: seasickness is no laugh and they proposed, as lunch time was approaching, to land on a little lonely island for a barbecue. Lunch sounded like a good idea to the colossus, so the captain headed for the island. Tough luck: 364 days a year that most beautiful and romantic tropical isle was deserted, but that day there was a party of twenty Italians having a barbecue. **"Is that your lonely island, is that what you call a tropical paradise?"** mocked the Duc, pouring scorn on Roland and the captain (he seemed to thrive on other people's mishaps).

Lunch passed fairly peacefully and was, as you would expect, prolonged by the Duc's various phone calls. So all in all there was little fishing time left and Roland suggested bottom-fishing in the hope that some sort of success would keep the Duc's mood at an acceptable level. The wind had died down and the sea was a flat calm: no problem for the ladies. While the boat boys were baiting the hooks, the Duc was shouting down his mobile. Some poor guy at the other end was given hell, and when everybody thought it couldn't get any worse, the choleric colossus threw the phone into the sea because the battery was dead. In the meantime the baited lines were out. Would they get round to fishing this time? No. Completely without warning, the giant nobleman jumped into the sea and announced snortingly as he surfaced that he wanted a swim. Those in the know were absolutely terrified: bait attracts sharks, and Roland and the captain ordered the Duc to get back on board immediately. He wouldn't hear of it. Laughing them off, he teasingly swam further away from the boat and was taken by a strong current. The captain had already given orders to pull the lines in and had started the engines. A buoy was thrown to the struggling swimmer, which he first refused to take, but eventually latched onto as he grew tired. He was heaved aboard, and everybody could see that he was as red as a lobster. One of the women remarked as much and the Duc now demanded the sunblock. Using a whole bottle, he covered himself with a thick layer of it then sat down on the stern bench. After about five minutes, trickles of sweat mixed with sun-cream ran down his enormous belly and dripped onto the deck. A really ugly picture – the crowning of a continuous insult on beauty. Rags in one place are riches in another: a complete lack of style. And how could there be any style? Without a minimal awareness of tradition there can be no style.

Traditional country life is a complex web of values which makes it so difficult to integrate people from other milieus in the countryside. There is no less tolerance or more racism in rural areas than elsewhere but definitely an aversion to a government prescribed radical multiculturalism. This is a problem all over Europe, and in my view surely the most symbolic of all episodes, incidents and statements relating to this powder-keg issue is the ruling by a German court that it is unacceptable for a Muslim girl to have to tolerate the presence of the cross in the classroom.

At the time of writing (October 2003) an Italian court has also ruled that in a school in Ofena the cross has to come down. Adel Smith, an Italian citizen and Muslim activist, filed a lawsuit challenging the legality of the cross in the classroom where his two sons attend. The judge ruled that: "the presence of the crucifix in classrooms communicates an implicit adherence to values that, in reality, are not the shared heritage of all citizens." (Source: Associated Press) On the basis of this the national flags of at least half of Europe's countries will have to go: the Swiss cross is even called a cross, so is the Scots, St. Andrew's cross, the Union Jack is a graphic union of crosses and all the Scandinavian countries will have to think of getting new flags as well. This is the reality of political correctness.

Thinking of crosses reminds me of the banks of the beautiful River Traun in Bavaria, where my cousin Theresa holds fishing rights. A footpath runs along the river, and every mile or so is a wayside cross, often richly decorated, and always well cared for, accompanying the walker or angler. What's it going to be: the chain saw or the axe? "What's this got to do with angling?" Bill immediately asks. The answer is: if the politically correct bunch can get away with removing crosses, they will eventually get away with a ban on fieldsports and angling.

If you think that here and there I am painting too gloomy a picture, just consider the fact that ten years ago nobody thought that hunting was going to be abolished, and in Scotland it has already happened. Hunting, shooting and fishing are on the agenda of urban politicians not just in Britain: **all over Europe and the USA there is a movement afoot to abolish country sports.**

NO
← FISHING →

The "hunting–shooting–fishing" ban sequence is the declared policy of the antis. If sportsmen fail to unite their forces on a long-term basis they are easy game for the antis, who will then proceed piecemeal. Hunting, shooting and fishing are symbolic pillars of country life. There is, however – and that is the main point – infinitely more at stake and more to traditional country life than hunting, shooting, fishing, wellies and tweed jackets.

Look at the Hook

Let's go back to angling basics: there is yet another angle which must be taken into consideration at the elementary level. It is that the action in hunting or trapping takes place in the same medium as human beings live in, whereas fishing takes place in an aquatic environment. An obvious point but, like many, of great consequence (the most obvious point and probably most important fact about British history, for example, is the Channel). When the ancient and modern angler casts his line, he casts it into an "alien" environment. He assumes certain things about the environment and the fish there, but he never really knows what is going to happen. Even to modern man there is still something awe-inspiring about a lake or the sea. Many people don't dare swim in a lake or the open sea for fear of being attacked by a monster; some beast that will take them down into the unknown dark. Reports of sea monsters make the headlines – to this very day – and Nessie is an evergreen. The world wouldn't be the same without it. Monsters and dragons have a long tradition: you'll find them in any culture anywhere since the dawn of time. Fishermen, though fully aware of potential mysteries, dangers and surprises try to haul up the facts: the fish. At the business end of the angler's fact-finding mission is the hook. No hook, no fish – but remember: no line, no fish; no knot, no fish.

The triad of hook, line and knot is inseparable for fishing purposes. Although necessary, it is however not sufficient to catch a fish. Fish, fisherman and some sort of bait are required at either end to start working and hoping for success. Hiding a hook in food (for example a worm) or dressing up a hook as food (as in fly fishing) seems to some people disgustingly deceitful. The reason for that is again a form of empathy. People don't like deceit and feel sorry for the poor fish who discovers that the juicy worm has a steely edge to it. As the saying goes, there is no such thing as a free lunch. Again, the fish doesn't believe anything of the sort and it can't be dejected by the deceitfulness of it all. **A fish is not a human being in disguise and must not be thought of as such.** If anti-anglers thought as consistently about fish as they do when talking about fishing, they would have to take the poor fish out of the cold water. After all, the wretches must be freezing to death, and aren't they in danger of drowning in all that water?

The line and the knot are just as "guilty" as the hook. Yet few people, not even anti-anglers, get their knickers in a twist about fishing line or fishing knots. Rope, string, cord or any knottable material and the corresponding knots are part of human culture in a wide variety of uses. And herein lies the difference to the fishing hook: while line and knots have myriads of applications, the fishing hook is always specifically a fishing hook. To anti-anglers the hook embodies all the reasons why they want to ban angling. Objectively, however, that ensemble of hook, line and knot was an epoch-making achievement and in fact the beginning of the modern world and of man's landing on the moon. If it's a symbol for anything, then it's surely one for our species' ingenuity, enterprise, will to improve and hope: hope to catch a fish and hope to find answers to life's conundrums.

I wouldn't have a snowball's chance in hell of catching a fish if each time I tied a hook to the line I were thinking about knot theory. Knot theory is a branch of mathematics the definition of which alone is mind-boggling:

...a knot is a single closed curve that meanders smoothly through Euclidian three-space without intersecting itself" (The History of Science and Knots).

It would take me many angling days to work that basic proposition out. Equally fatal to my angling prospects would be reflections on the history of knots, that is, all the way from the first knot to knot theory. Just a cursory glance at this knotty topic reveals how deeply seated in human culture knots are. Think of knots used as messages, as a means of bookkeeping; think of knots in string games, weaving, decoration, science and art – there can't be many knotless human activities. Knots even play into thinking when you ponder knotty issues. Anyway, on the applied side there is the elementary equation which every angler has fully understood since the dawn of time: bad knot = fish lost.

62

Knots are tied with intention

Knots are tied with intention but not all knots are intention

Knots are tied with intention but not all knots are intention

Knots are tied with intention

ot all knots are intentional

knots are intentional

Wind knots and tangles are unintentional, involuntary knots. There is however a suggestion of agency in the "wind knot", and I quite fancy the idea of Boreas (N), Notus (S), Eurus (E) and Zephyrus (W), the Greek wind gods, artfully blowing a knot into the leader and having a good laugh at the expense of the angler. A simple wind knot looks like a minor annoyance but is a major nuisance and what's more: that little knot in the leader is just not right and weakens it. It's aesthetically displeasing; it's like a blot in the landscape. Always remove it. Tangles are usually also of Greek origin, and for a better understanding of the phenomenon, it is always helpful to consider McGillicuddy's famous laws of tangles:

The first law of tangles is that it is dead easy to get yourself into a tangle.

The second law of tangles is that fish take left, right and centre while you disentangle.

The third law of tangles is that when you're ready again, the action is over.

Helpful as these laws are for the understanding of tangles, there is a lot of uncharted territory in the universe of chaos and confusion. Take the classic case of the seemingly simple tangle which you hope to disentangle by giving it a tug at one end. This results either in a tight knot or, by some magic, a new tangle of mind-boggling dimensions. In fact I suspect that getting from a tangle into a worse tangle is even easier than getting into the initial tangle. Similar to this is the situation of the line wound around the rod tip, which is an embryonic tangle, so to speak. With a few flicks you try to unwind it. The very moment you do that, a gust plants you with a fully grown tangle.

While McGillicuddy's first law is universally acknowledged as unshakeable fact and truth, the second law has raised some criticisms on the grounds that it is not always the case that fish become active during a tangle. On a big lake, for example, with a great number of boats and fishermen and with changing winds, there is bound to be a tangle somewhere on the lake at any moment during the fishing day. The critics point out that under such a constellation, fish should be active all day, which they clearly never are. The second law comprises, however, a range of subtleties which escapes its critics. The law doesn't specify the precise area where the fish take when the angler is disentangling. To McGillicuddy it seemed obvious, however, that the area in question was that in the vicinity of the angler, i.e. where (were he not tangled) the angler could have easily cast his fly. "Ah", you say, but I have had a tangle, and the fish weren't suddenly triggered into action near me or anywhere else. This objection looks like a heavy blow to the second law, but consider the following:

1) While occupied by your tangle, how can you be sure you're actually seeing all that goes on around you? The second law clearly states, "while you disentangle".

2) Be honest: the moment you get yourself into a tangle you get annoyed. The reason for the annoyance can be none other than the fact that deep down, you and every other angler think something like "the cast I am missing now would have raised a fish". In other words, you *think* fish are active. The beauty of the second law is that it covers the factual and psychological dimensions with equal elegance. And now have a look at the third law: of course, the particular action that was taking place while you were disentangling is irretrievably lost because whatever follows after the tangle is new action, i.e. fish getting active when you're not tangled. This, you might be tempted to think, borders on sophistry, but I assure you that the more objections you're trying to find to McGillicuddy's laws, the more their validity becomes apparent.

Much as I appreciate and even admire the clarity of McGillicuddy's laws, I have always sensed a slightly pessimistic slant in them. Compare now Hugh Falkus's thoughts on tangles, which are a mix of "Damn" (or stronger) and a down-to-earth "Let's solve this problem" approach:

Tangles are the curse of angling and darken the lives of all anglers from time to time. Don't despair. Most tangles are easy to unravel once you know the secret. It is this: almost all tangles are caused by loops of line getting caught up. Work round the tangle, freeing these loops. Provided the line is not pulled too tight, there is no tangle that will not unravel in a few minutes. The golden rules are:

1. Patience.
2. Don't pull.
3. Find the loops and free them one by one.

When you have freed all the loops the tangle will be undone.

McGillicuddy's laws, being natural laws, can't be bothered with curses or bias; if there is something in them which we perceive as inexorable, then that is merely part of their nature. Nevertheless, why not look at tangles from other angles; why not shift the point of view completely and ask, for example, "is there something good about a tangle?" Is there perhaps something which takes the sting out of the curse? Are they a curse in the first place? Is there something McGillicuddy and Falkus have missed?

I once fished with a pipe-smoking Japanese angler for trout on a Loch in the Scottish Highlands. The wind was tangly, i.e. it came in from all directions at the same time and occasionally the forward cast came straight back without touching the water. All in all fairly bumpy but still fishable. So, not surprisingly, I got myself into a specimen tangle. I must have muttered something or other because my companion glanced at me, saw the tangle and motioned that I should move the rod so that he could have a look at it.

Like a blackbird prospecting for worms, he inclined his head slightly sideways and scrutinised the tangle. Then, with incredible dexterity and purpose – there was absolutely nothing tentative about his pulls and turns – he unravelled in no time what had looked to me a lost cause. And for good measure he simultaneously relit his pipe (with a lighter) and then gave me one of those inscrutable smiles. I was flabbergasted, speechless and full of admiration for my companion, and while fishing away, I wondered about him. Was he a Zen monk or master of some meditative or martial art? But would they smoke pipes? Whatever, it was absolutely stunning – great! The bad news is that this level is beyond our reach – beyond mine anyway. To get there you need to start in kindergarten or even well before that. So what's the good news?

If you calculate your chances of catching a fish quantitatively, it seems indeed that a tangle diminishes the likelihood of success. When the hook and the bait are in the water they fish; when they're out they don't. Qualitatively speaking, things present themselves differently if you take a different attitude to the tangle altogether. The best things in life come free, and the tangle is one of them. Instead of chagrined silent swearing, say to yourself, "Wow, I've got a tangle!" and then take the JPSA (Japanese Pipe Smoker Approach) which basically means appreciating the beauty of it. Yes, the beauty. A masterpiece of knotting exclusively blown together for you by the Greek wind gods. Look closely at the intricate wind artwork which often cocoons your flies in line. There is a mysterious quality to some of the highly complex tangles which on closer analysis turn out to be incredibly easy to unravel. Most tangles, though, behave like tangles: they pose a problem, but by the aesthetically positive JPSA approach, you take the sting out of them regardless whether you determinedly work your way out of the tangle or whether you rig up from scratch. Why?

By assessing the tangle in an aesthetically positive way you can begin to understand its intricacies better and identify more clearly the best course of action. Just let me illustrate the opposite: by getting annoyed (instead of agreeably surprised) by the tangle and inwardly cursing it, you take a hostile attitude to it. Even worse, some anglers sulk. All this takes time, whereas a positive "Ah, look what a beauty I've got here" is guided by a lively interest and a correspondingly quick solution to the problem. The JPSA is also more relaxing. If you let yourself be negatively taken in by the tangle, you tend to get tense, which shows later when you're fishing: your presentation suffers, your powers of observation diminish, the timing of your strikes fails...

In short, your rhythm is broken and you catch no fish. By being positive in the JPSA sense, you come out of the tangle relaxed with the result that your offering is impeccable, your eye is keener and your reflexes sharpened. You catch fish and at the same time become an expert on the beauty of tangles, which in itself is a pleasure and a good thing.

I have said above that the elementary equation 'bad knot = fish lost' is known to every angler. It is, however, undoubtedly the case that this solid piece of knowledge is often ignored. Anglers the world over lose fish on account of bad knots. The reason for this is that applying knowledge is more difficult than one would assume at first glance. Take lying, for example. Everybody knows that lying is basically wrong; yet if the lies of politicians were to change to snowflakes, there would be daily blizzards even in the deserts. Likewise, there are many knot rush-jobs every day which lose fish.

Typically when setting up the gear, anglers tend to hurry when they see fish jump – their angling urge gets the better of them. Typically also, anglers who hurry will make a mess of their knots. Then there is carelessness, absent-mindedness, momentary distraction and many other reasons which contribute more or less heavily to a bad knot. Applying knowledge is an art that can be learned and requires a bit of discipline, but with the right attitude as in JPSA the exercise is not only a pleasure but will also catch you more fish. Applying "knotledge" will make you a better fisherman.

"A good knot looks good," says Peter Owen in his *Pocket Guide to Fishing Knots*. And a good knot feels good. The best knot is the one you have confidence in. The source of that confidence is the proper, concentrated application of your knotting knowledge, which will spare you the calamitous experience of losing a fish because of a bad knot.

Roland Pertwee summarises the situation regarding the bad knot with great lucidity (*Fisherman's Bounty*):

Your true-born angler does not go blindly to work until he has first satisfied his conscience. There is a pride in knots of which the laity knows nothing, and if, through neglect to tie them rightly, failure and loss should result, pride may not be restored nor conscience salved by the plea of eagerness.

There are, to be sure, many other reasons why fish get away. Some of them can be quite unexpected. Every year many a fine fish is lost, for example, to mink. In regions where minks roam freely, courtesy of animal-rights morons who "liberated" them, the angler is well advised not to let his catch lie on the bank unsecured. Before he can count to ten, the fish is gone. This is a relatively straightforward way of losing a fish at the last minute. Before I tell you about a most extraordinary sequence of events, I have to say that you should use the expression "losing a fish" with some reservation. As Izaak Walton remarked, "no man can lose what he never had". So on the understanding that I am using the word "lose" in a loose sense, here follows the account of my most stunning loss of a fish.

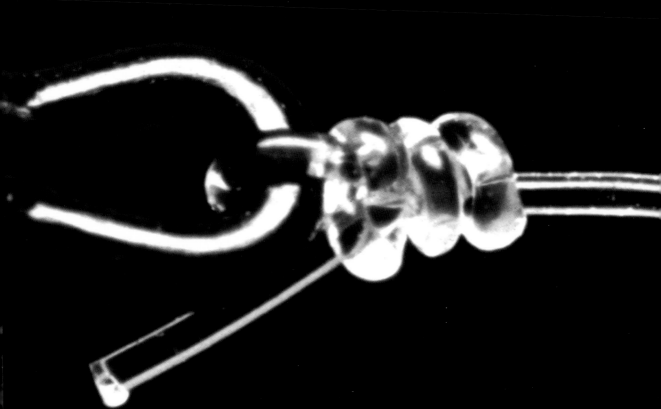

The fish in question was a dorado caught on the fly off the island of Mahé in the Seychelles. My friend and guide Roland Henrion and I were fishing loch style from his little boat just off the reef when, shortly before we had to call it a day, the dorado took. It was a little golden beauty, which comfortably filled the silver plate on which it was served. We – Sophie (Roland's wife), Roland, my wife Regina and myself – sat in the elegant seafront terrace restaurant of the Sunset Beach Hotel. As it was close to Christmas, the hotel was full and around us all the tables hummed. The restaurant, an extension of the main building, was half covered by a thatched roof, so roughly half the tables were truly open air and the others under the roof. Imagine the scene: beautifully set tables, elegant people, breathtaking tropical scenery, the gentle sound of the waves, wafts of tropical scents, just that and a little breeze making the temperature comfortable. Just before the night suddenly set in, the candles on the tables were lit. With the starters served and the apéritifs doing their job, the conversations intensified and created a gently animated atmosphere. There is a magic in that kind of soft tropical night which you can't escape. Just about everything seems right, is right, and that dorado would be the icing on the cake.

At the table next to us was a young couple, probably on their honeymoon and certainly deeply in love: they had eyes and ears only for each other. But even they briefly looked up when the dorado was presented. It was lovingly prepared, decorated with flowers, and the hotel manager and his assistants gave it just the right amount of ceremony, showing it to us and then putting it on a serving trolley beside the table. As the head waiter smilingly took a spoon and a fork in order to prepare the servings, a dull thud made cutlery, plates and glasses jump, and for a second everybody, including the rat that had landed on our table, was petrified. There it was in the middle of the table: a huge, fat rat. I hadn't seen anything like it before. Our table was right underneath the edge of the thatched roof…

It shook off its shock and then bolted – the path it chose led over the silver plate, and, in passing it actually grabbed the dorado and jumped with it to the floor. This made the silver plate fall with a clatter, waking everybody from their paralysis, and the commotion that followed would have done any action movie proud. Rat and fish went straight under the table of the lovebirds, and the poor young woman fainted. The rat didn't know how to get out of the restaurant, it had to look for an exit. This meant running to and fro under practically every table, leaving havoc in its trail. It finally found its way out, but the turmoil created in just over thirty seconds was considerable. Worst of all, from our point of view, was the loss of the dorado: bits and pieces of it were all over the restaurant floor – what a sad sight, what a shame, what a way to lose a fish. After the initial shock, everybody recovered in relatively little time. More than anything else, the incident had an animating effect: for many the evening stretched into a long night with free after-dinner drinks.

Back to knots: "A good knot looks good" is also the springboard for a series of completely different problems regarding knots. The knot looks good and feels good because you have tied it in accordance with the rules and knowledge that govern fishing-knot tying. So far, so good, but there's more: the medium of the knot is a line. For the caveman as well as modern man, the line would be of some vegetable material (e.g. raffia, string) or animal material (e.g. horsehair, gut, braided silk). In the 1960s monofilament replaced the natural materials, but it didn't replace that piece of ancient knowledge: the knot. Unless some revolutionary welding technique is invented, the knot will remain a part of angling as long as the latter exists.

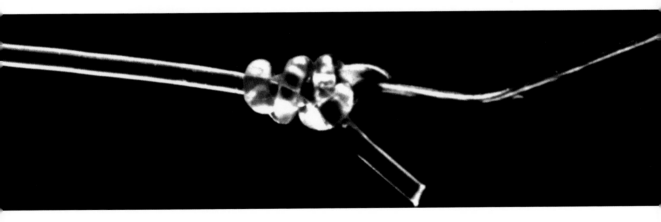

Tie a hook to the line, then get a magnifying glass and have a look at the knot. Look at it from various angles, change the light and the background a bit and you'll discover that **the transparent, cold monofilament looks like an ice sculpture.** The way the twists and turns of a good knot are arranged is positively pleasing. There is proportion, there is a self-evidence about a good knot which is just beautiful. Beholding and searching for beauty is a pleasure. There seems to be a strong link between the good (knot) and the beautiful. In the case of the knot, the source of the good, i.e. the beautiful, is that the knot in question fulfils its functionality to perfection. What's the point, you'll be asking yourself at this juncture? Well, **by looking for beauty and the good, you're looking last but not least for knowledge** about the reality of the world.

If this strikes you as vague and *démodé,* which it probably does, then have a look at these names: Kepler, Einstein, Heisenberg, Poincaré, Cricks and Watson (DNA), Dirac, Weinberg, Chandrashekar and so on. All these giants of science acknowledge and look for beauty and truth in mathematics, biology and physics. Critics of "beauty in science" will claim that those scientists who see beauty just get carried away and that beauty has absolutely no place in science. They will moreover claim that beauty is positively an obstacle to new findings and the progress of science. They will point out that some cosmological theories, for example, have been called beautiful and then faulted and subsequently revised. Einstein is an often cited case. He is said to have assumed on the basis of "scientific aestheticism" that the universe is static and later to have had to correct his views in that respect. Nevertheless, Steven Weinberg, a physics Nobel laureate, remarked recently that if ever there were an all-encompassing theory or formula about the world, you would recognise it by its beauty.

What is really so objectionable about beauty and God in science and elsewhere? The crux is that the beauty referred to by those scientists and the beauty I refer to in angling is a concept which involves the notions of symmetry, harmony, order, goodness and truth. This classical idea goes against the grain of so-called progressive philosophers who would like to see beauty fragmentised. Fragmentation means that beauty isn't seen as an objective entity but more in terms of subjective experience: beauty is in the eye of the beholder.

Beauty in a classical sense is a thorn in the flesh of lifestyle thinkers because it involves values which link it to Christianity. Christianity, in particular, and God in general are accused of standing in the way of a perfectly scientific and rational new world. There are historians, philosophers - indeed whole university establishments - whose sole task seems to be to carp, belittle and insult Christianity and Christian tradition. Nevertheless it shows remarkable and encouraging resilience. Moreover, an open-minded look at the history of science shows a different picture from that painted by the gravediggers of Western culture: Why, for example, is it that the scientifically most advanced societies are Christian? Why, for example, are Western societies the most open and tolerant? Why, for example, are Western countries the most desirable for immigration?

The obvious is often easily overlooked or hard to understand. The one most basic fact of the human condition is God. Intelligent materialists like Wilson (the biologist) readily acknowledge that. They then go on to say God is a genetically pre-programmed disposition in man, and once we recognise this we can nudge that disposition in any way we want in order to see God in the "right" things. What we have here is scientific materialism with scientists as priests. I think this is in many ways wrong but the most important flaw is that God is presented as natural-material (the gene) whereas God by definition is supernatural.

Cosmological theories attempt to unravel the complexities of the universe: there have been many bold constructs and there will be many more to come. But whatever their findings, there will still be one final Why? When all material aspects have been elucidated, there will still be some open questions. Let's have a quick look at the Big Bang theory, which is at present the most widely accepted view of how the universe formed. The Big Bang theory states that at some point 10 to 20 billion years ago, there was a cosmic explosion hurling matter in all directions. That matter coalesced into the galaxies racing away from us – well, whatever the nuts and bolts of it, the really essential questions are why and where from? If indeed it was like the theory says, why was that matter there in the first place and where did it come from? If you answer these questions with reference to other matter, i.e. there was original matter out of which the exploding matter was generated and so on, then, logically, there must be somewhere along the line a prime cause, a prime mover. That prime mover is God. There is nothing mysterious or nebulous about that. It is perfectly logical and rational to say there is a God.

Back to the hook: I said its beauty is in its simplicity. This simplicity is deceptive in as much as it hides an immense number of relations participating in and constituting that simplicity. Objects of similar simplicity (and complexity) are, for example, the wheel and the screw. The hook is a beautiful object because it unites perfection in craft, functionality, simplicity and proportion; and the fact that it has been used since time immemorial adds a quality to it which can't be found in many other objects. On the emotional level, its utility pleases. But today the hook never rouses emotions like a rod does. The same goes for the line. I doubt that many anglers are emotionally stirred by their lines unless they get broken by a big fish. This event usually triggers off strong emotions and deep reflections about the line and makes anglers more "line conscious". I said that

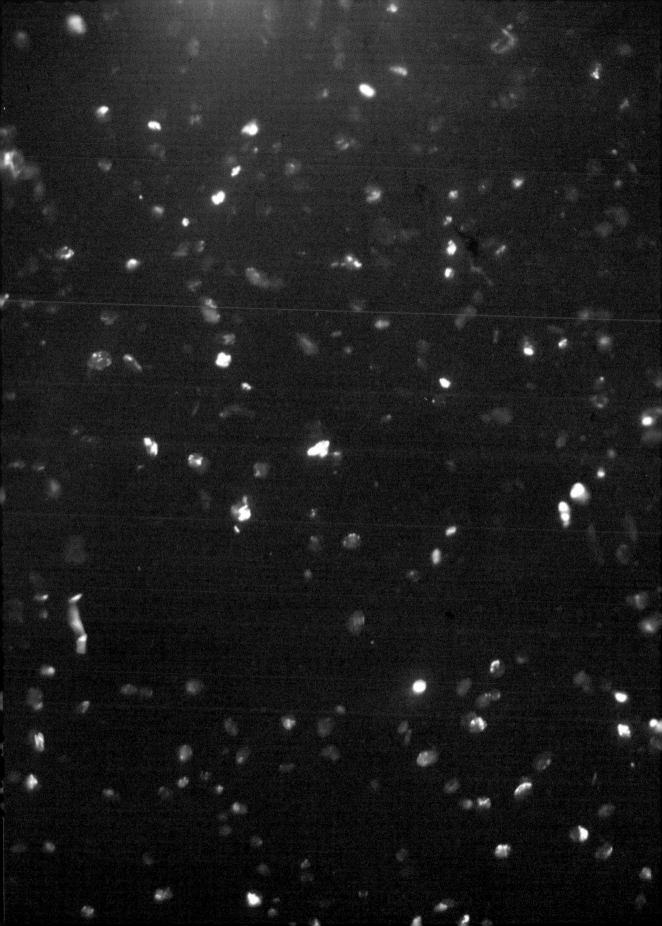

hook and line were the wallflowers in the tackle shop – and what beautiful flowers they turn out to be. On closer inspection, the line reveals the same qualities as the hook. The perfection in production: modern monofilament lines can't be faulted on that score or under the aspect of simplicity. If you dabble a bit with polymer chemistry (no problem on the internet) and then appreciate the line from that angle, an absolutely fascinating universe opens. In the apparent simplicity of a modern line resides a wonderful body of chemical and mathematical knowledge.

Beauty is a fact of life. All societies over the ages have had their own ideas about beauty in nature (flowers), in objects (knots), in human beings (women), and in actions (football, moral actions). You'll notice that I don't mention art – I'll get to that shortly. No doubt, not everybody will immediately see the beauty of your perfectly tied Grinner knot, but the person not seeing beauty in the Grinner might recognise it in crochet work or the knot drawings in the Book of Kells, for which in turn you have no eye. Or, to put it precisely, no trained eye. There are aspects of beauty which if you don't discover yourself can be learned about.

Once you know what to look for, you spot the required qualities immediately. In the fishing knot, you're looking beyond the rules that govern a particular knot (and all knots) for proportion and self-evidence. If you find these qualities in a knot, you know it's a beautiful knot because it has a perfection which pleases the senses and the intellect. You know you have an instance of beauty before you. The beauty of a flower is grasped by most people intuitively. The beauty of the flower is understood without reference to proportion, self-evidence or functionality – even though these qualities are, of course, present. **Beauty, however, is not just the sum of certain qualities but their unity.** That unity is perfection. That is why when you behold beauty, you're always looking at an instance of the same thing regardless of how different the objects or actions are in which you perceive it. It's like love. Love, apart from its particular "occurrences" is a universal reality. Beauty, in other words, is a glimpse of perfection. These glimpses can be had by everyone, beauty (like love) being universally accessible – there are absolutely no conditions attached to perfection.

I have to tell you a story here: There was once a girl working at a village petrol station somewhere near a fishing haunt of mine. By all present-day standards that girl was plain ugly. Too fat, too many hormones of the wrong kind, pimples – she was everything a girl doesn't want to be. Probably to make the best of it, she celebrated the fact by dressing in a way, which emphasised her "imperfections" and cultivated a hate-and-spite attitude. She had a well-trained evil stare which sent shivers down the spines of unsuspecting first-time customers. She knew, and I suspect was very pleased with, the effect.

One day I went for petrol and took a bottle of mineral water out of the sales fridge and handed it over to her. She moved the recently introduced scanner over it: nothing doing. Once more, twice more, then she held the scanner right in front of her, gave it her evil stare and screamed at it. It was a blood-curdling scream so loud it would have drowned low-flying jumbo jet, and had there been a churchyard nearby, it would have awakened the dead. I stood there petrified watching her move the scanner over the code again. The bleep signalled that the magic had worked. She looked at me triumphantly and in a matter-of-fact voice stated: "I can scare the shit out of anything", upon which I burst into a hysteric fit of laughter. And then the absolutely unexpected happened: she smiled; nay, she radiated, she beamed happiness. She was completely relaxed and then she joined in my laughter and we both slapped our thighs, tears rolling down our cheeks. Even when the eruption of mirth was over, she still smiled and, honestly, she didn't look the slightest bit ugly. For a moment that girl was positively beautiful, but alas she soon fell back into her grimness in which she looked her self-imposed ugly self again. Nevertheless, there had been a moment of beauty. Although it is clear that beauty exists, it is far from clear how and where you can find it.

At this juncture I have to focus briefly on art, because with expressions such as "aesthetically pleasing" I have at least in terminology moved close to that realm and philosophy. The term and the study of aesthetics was invented by Alexander Gottlieb Baumgarten in the mid-18th century. The term, according to Baumgarten, is originally Greek and can mean "to perceive" or "to feel", and consequently he defined aesthetics as "the science of sensory cognition". What's the big deal? As such, as Baumgarten himself recognised, there is nothing new in the idea, but to make sensory cognition a subject was novel. To fully understand this, it is helpful to look at the antonym of aesthetic: anaesthetic. Anaesthetisation switches perception off, so to speak. In an anaesthetic state, no knowledge can be gained. Aesthetic is the opposite pole, when all senses function well and are able to perceive. "Aesthetics" tries to work out how we can gain knowledge through perception. Baumgarten distinguished knowledge gained from perception and the representation of such knowledge in painting and poetry, i.e. the arts. The study of the representations evolved into what today should be called "philosophy of art" rather than aesthetics. Aesthetics is historically tied to beauty (because at the time of Baumgarten's invention of aesthetics the beautiful was all important).

Art in the contemporary sense doesn't play into the basic fishing situation. What, you'll be wondering is art in the contemporary sense? I don't know exactly, but most of it seems little concerned with beauty and skill. Let me give you an idea of what I mean by "modern art": I sketch you the background of one example. Somebody somewhere diagnosed a lack of culture in rural areas and persuaded the local authorities to sponsor a fund for art projects in their regions: "Art in Rural Space". What you need to know is that country folk, especially the small farmers here in Switzerland, are having a hard time at present. The economic pressure on them is intense and there are a host of other problems on the employment side. But never mind, art it had to be. One of the award-winning projects (£2,000) involved dropping a dead horse from a helicopter onto a tractor. According to the "artists", the meaning of this sculpture (sic) was to show that the unimaginable can become real. Wow! The village on which this sculpture should have been dropped protested, and their predictable anger was presumably also part of the project. After all, press reports of upset villagers would enhance urban artistic careers. The villagers were simply cannon fodder in the artists' march to fame. Disgusting. The "art" here consists in selling the brainless, the exploitative and the misanthropic as art. That is the sort of thing I mean when I say "modern art", which remarkably resembles modern morals where wrong is right, bad is good and ugly is beautiful. I have just learned from the newspapers that the "artists" in question were awarded the "Cultural achievement of the year" award by the town they live in.

In *The Compleat Angler*, Izaak Walton (1593–1683) uses the word "art" frequently and at one point explains:

O sir, doubt not that angling is an art. Is it not an art to deceive a trout with an artificial fly?

Walton uses "art" in the sense of something well and skilfully done. The perception of the artist as a creator of beautiful works is one of the achievements of the Renaissance. The Renaissance discovered artists, or perhaps it is more accurate to say that artists discovered themselves. They created in the sense that by imitating nature they created something new. The special status of the artist was not known in mediaeval times. Mediaeval "artists" were craftsmen translating religious and metaphysical meanings into sculptures and pictures. They weren't seen to create. It's rather like translators today: they are not usually credited with creative powers and so enjoy no special status. The fisherman uses his art in the sense that he applies his knowledge to catch fish: the fisherman doesn't create like an artist does.

Angling is a participant's sport in more than one sense of the word. Angling is embedded in nature; the angler is integrated into the beauty of nature. The beauty of nature? It is universally agreed that nature is beautiful, but what exactly is meant by "the beauty of nature"? I wonder about our caveman who discovered the hook. Did he think nature was beautiful? To him, nature could

have looked more like an evil fate posing all sorts of demanding challenges, forcing him into a brutal struggle for survival. One could plausibly assume that there was no time, no leisure, and no need for beauty. But being human, our man surely had a sense of beauty – recognising perfection in a particularly fine trout or whatever he fished for. And couldn't those little moments when he stopped to admire, contemplate and wonder – whatever the appropriate word – have been the basis of new discoveries and improvements? In other words, if the caveman had had an absolutely unreflective nature, he wouldn't have made any progress at all. Man can't help thinking of nature as beautiful because it simply is beautiful. That is what "the beauty of nature" means. The caveman might have expressed the fact differently, but fact it was then as now. Equally indisputable is the fact that many a caveman must have enjoyed fishing in the sense of getting pleasure out of it. Fishing was a necessity but necessity does not automatically exclude pleasure, a point which emphasises my earlier conclusion that angling has always been good.

I have said that the angler integrates into the beauty of nature simply by being part of the physical world. That is one way in which he *nolens volens* is a participant. The second way is that the angler participates in a sport in the sense that he abides by rules and conventions governing the activity. **Angling isn't about yanking out fish at all costs by all means but catching them according to the book and for pleasure.** The deeper meaning of the rules and conventions is that they order the activity into do's and don'ts, thereby giving it a moral content. Teaching youngsters to fish also means moral teaching in the most elementary sense that there are such things as values. Likewise, introducing young people to fishing means telling them about nature's ways, thereby showing them the way to the beauty of nature, enabling them to see beauty. If you prefer a version with a materialist ring to it, you could also say angling is applied natural history and natural science.

The perception of angling has long had an emphatically bucolic and romantic side to it. In fact, the angler or the image of an angler is the epitome of tranquillity and peace. This archetypal image has been cemented over the centuries since *The Compleat Angler*. In his superb book *Angling in Art*, Tom Quinn presents the imagery of angling through the centuries. In the following passage, he analyses the status of the angler in paintings around the time when Izaak Walton wrote *The Compleat Angler*:

In the pastoral landscapes painted by a number of Dutch, French and Italian painters the angler is occasionally given a role as an idealised detail in an ideal landscape. A good example is Nicolas Poussin's 'Landscape with Orpheus and Eurydice' (1650), showing Orpheus with Eurydice at the moment when she is about to be poisoned by a snake. The scene is one of gilded youth awaiting tragedy. But just behind the main figures is an angler whose role in the picture is clearly to suggest the peace and tranquillity that is about to end. His rustic presence, however insignificant a part it may play in the central meaning of the painting, nonetheless indicates the increasing importance of the angler as a symbol of tranquillity, a symbol of the individual removed from the cares of the world. As such the angler is a perfect, if unsophisticated focus of interest in many paintings.

I think there is more to that angler than meets the eye. Poussin's angler is practically in the middle of that picture, in the most conspicuous place. He looks over his shoulder at the scene. Consider now the story of Orpheus and Eurydice in bare outline: Orpheus was famous for playing the lyre. Nobody and nothing could withstand the charm of his music. Eurydice dies and disappears into the underworld. Orpheus plays the lyre and sings his grief to the deities of the underworld, who are so moved that they agree to return Eurydice to him and this world. On one condition: when leaving the underworld together with Eurydice, Orpheus is not to look back until they are in the real world again. Orpheus looks back, and Eurydice dies a second time but there is no second deal with the rulers of the underworld. Orpheus loses Eurydice forever. Now think about that angler again. By looking back over his shoulder he will miss the fish that takes at the very moment when he is being distracted by the events behind him. The angler is the whole story of Orpheus and Eurydice in a nutshell. In an age when painters were obsessed with detail, the choice of the angler in the centre of the picture in that pose must have been fully intentional. Either Poussin was an angler himself or he knew a good deal about angling. The angler there is more than "the symbol of tranquillity"; he is the story doubled.

SHOOTING CHUB

Any search for beauty must, if simply for the sake of completeness, look at ugliness. Some ugly zones of angling are easily identified: they are those which involve the breaking of laws, rules and customs, written and unwritten. The sporting world over, deliberate foul-hooking, for example, is banished because it's wrong, it's ugly. Littering and discarding line, although universally accepted to be bad, still "breaks out" here and there in the places I fish and is aesthetically unacceptable: it's wrong, it's ugly. Laws and rules help to promote beauty, but it is sometimes hard to see that they do.

In 1966 I was fined the phenomenal sum of 10 Swiss francs for fishing "with artificial bait", an injustice I strongly resent to this day. The facts were straightforward. The "small" fishing permit I held allowed "fishing with natural bait" only; Fishing with "artificial bait", e.g. spoons (fly fishing was unheard of), was the privilege of those with the "big" permit, which was outside my reach. Of course, I was under the foolish illusion that if only I could fish with a spoon, I would catch more and bigger fish. That type of foolishness I carried a long way into my fishing life until I finally learnt that expensive fishing doesn't necessarily mean good or better fishing. Instead of spoons, fishermen with the "small" permit used slugs, which, if you put a swivel in the line, turned like spoons. This didn't satisfy me and I considered painting slugs. Apart from presenting a technical problem, however, this would, by virtue of the colour, turn the slug into at least half an artificial bait.

So the idea I finally hit on was orange peel. A small section of orange peel would turn on a hook like a spoon. In order to get it down to fishing depth the lead (shot) had to be put right on the big hook or just above the hook – and I wasn't sure how to do this. Finally, one Wednesday afternoon (no school) I decided to put the theory into practice. I tried various unsatisfactory versions – the orange peel had tended to fall off when cast too hard or else it slipped down the hook shank – but even before I had found a fishable solution, one of the bailiffs stood beside me. So absorbed was I that I hadn't heard him approaching. I didn't mind, either way: my conscience was clear, I had my little permit with me and I had nothing to hide. "That is artificial bait," he said, "Orange peel is natural," I said but I didn't, of course, stand a chance.

Apart from being a stupid, narrow-minded human being, that saphead was, of course, vested with the authority to fine me. To cut a long story short, the idiot confiscated my hook, line, orange peel and sinker, and it all ended in tears, frustration and anger. Then a week later, to the shock of my parents, the letter from the police said that I had violated Article such and such section such and such, and that the fine for that would be 10 francs. They paid up. The alternative would have been a lengthy appeal costing money, time, contacts, patience, nerves and knowledge, none of which we had. Unfortunately – because the man shouldn't have got away with it. I do bear grudges – not many, but those I do bear, I look after well.

Justitia, the Roman goddess of Justice, might have had her day off but *Nemesis*, the Greek goddess of retribution, was on duty. And she chose the Coleman brothers as her executors. The three of them were a bit older than I, and all of them fished often not for pleasure but to put food on the table. By any modern standard they were poor. One evening that same moron bailiff tried to nail them on some petty matter (I think it was for standing in the water. With the "little" permit you were allowed to fish from the bank only. So standing on a stone in the water, you're not fishing from the bank...). He announced a fine of 30 francs, which to them was a fortune. They would never be able to pay that, meaning they would have to go to prison if bad came to worse. With our man there was no reasoning and consequently the Colemans took matters into their own strong hands.

It was towards evening, no witnesses. Driven by hopelessness, they threw him in the river, which luckily wasn't very deep there. Soaked, he stood up and threatened them with more fines, prison and what not, which intensified the brothers' despair beyond endurance. They waded out and dunked him a couple of times until he swore not to fine them and not to report them to the police. The nincompoop was as good as his word – even better: he resigned. How do I know that, you ask? One of the brothers told me and I have no reason to doubt his word.

All this is definitely not beautiful. It's got nothing to do with the beauty of angling. The less conflict there is at the waterside, the better. Enlightened rules and intelligent enforcement help. I think in that respect progress has been made because it has been understood that young anglers should be encouraged rather than frightened off. "Rarity is the precursor to extinction," Darwin said and how obviously true: **the fewer anglers there are, the higher the risk of angling being marginalised and then abolished.**

Talking of margins, I have to tell you about Max. After his apprenticeship as a gardener, Max worked on a freelance basis for his former employer. We hadn't seen him in the pub for about a week, which wasn't unusual because he was away on a job. Then, one evening, Max and his boss turned up and after the usual greeting banter, he joined the conversation and told us where he had been. Nobody had heard of that Alpine foothills village, which was about three-hours' drive away. Nor did anybody know of the small lake that was just half an hour's walk beyond that. "Beautiful lake..." said Max dreamily, gazing intently at the ceiling as if he could see the lake there; and then, as if describing the location of a treasure, he added in a conspiratorial stage whisper "... and full of trout – which reminds me: I must go and get them and put them in the fridge."

What he meant was, put them in the landlord's fridge. You see, Max was living at many places and nowhere in particular. Sometimes he was with his parents, sometimes with friends, sometimes with his brother, sometimes with his sister and sometimes, especially in summer, in the meadows. Most of the time, however, he was looked after or provided for by women of all stations and ages. He was a great ladies' man: they adored him, they loved him, they fell for him. There was something in his eyes which made them tolerate what they would immediately object to in another man. He didn't give a fig about his appearance (mind you, he was never shabby), and his footloose and fancy-free lifestyle wasn't exactly trust-inspiring. They also generously overlooked the Gauloise Bleu glued (and removed only to be replaced by a joint) to the corner of his mouth, and he wasn't an alcoholic: he was pure alcohol. His nutritional requirements were liquid and his appetite enormous. I don't think I have ever seen him eat anything. This way of life would have killed an ordinary man within a year but didn't seem to affect him at all. In all his incredible excess his physical and intellectual powers never deserted him. He was an intelligent, amiable bloke full of good humour and wit and, beyond that, a fisherman nobody could hold a candle to.

So out he went to get the trout. They were half a dozen lovely rainbows about a pound and a half each. Having duly admired them, we were eager to learn more. Max had our undivided attention and he related in vivid detail the glories of that lake and made a point of mentioning that they had eaten trout all week – Max's boss confirmed this with an emphatic nod. It was enough to convince Henry and me to give that lake a try the very next day, which was a Saturday. So where would we get a permit? "That's easy," said Max. "If you're there before the post office opens, you put a notice with your car number plate in the letter box and then when you return in the evening you pay there." He then drew a little map of the lake on a beer mat, highlighting the good spots. Equipped with the beer mat and a road map borrowed from the landlord, we set off the following morning at 3.30. We arrived at the village three hours later. It was a crisp, beautiful, promising Alpine morning. We

90

considered ourselves lucky that there were no cars yet at the post office, so we would have the lake all to ourselves – at least to begin with. We put the note in the letterbox, got our gear out and headed off for the lake. Finding the track was no problem because it was signposted right behind the post office, just as Max had said it would be. Exactly half an hour later we reached the lake – the reservoir to be precise. It was empty. Practically empty: there were little trickles of melting snow and a puddle in front of the sluices, but it was clear there couldn't possibly be any fish in it – no point in consulting the beer mat for the hot spots.

We were stunned. Dumbfounded, we made our way back to the post-office car park. Having slightly recovered, we reasoned that they had emptied the reservoir for maintenance or security reasons. Back at the car park, we met the man from the post office to whom we related our plight, upon which he broke out in convulsions of laughter. We were worried for his health and didn't think there was anything funny. Not at all. "D..d…d…d..dooo…whatt….t…da…da…da…y..y…y…y…y…iiiiiiiit is?" the man managed to stammer. "Saturday," we answered simultaneously, which brought about a new fit of laughter – tears were now freely flowing over the man's cheeks. After a while the laughter subsided and he managed to inform us that there had never been fish in that reservoir and that it was April 1st, April Fools' Day.

Neither I nor my colleague Henry had ever been so beautifully had, and, to our credit, I am happy to add that we fully appreciated it. The return of the fools to the pub was some event, I can tell you, and Max was extremely pleased with himself and deserved all the pints we treated him to. The trout, by the way, were his main worry, he told us. He feared we would spot their identical size and condition – he had "obtained" them from a nearby trout farm – but there he had clearly over-estimated our powers of piscatorial perception and, on top of that, we were blinded by our eagerness and angling urge.

It was a scorcher; a shimmery heat rose from the meadows as I lay dozing under a tree. All life was half asleep. Even midges and horseflies hid somewhere cool. "Bang, bang, bang!" the unmistakable sound of shots made me sit up abruptly. Again "Bang, bang, bang!"

in semi-automatic staccato from the other bank. Then silence and a couple of minutes later rapid fire. Then all went quiet again, and with my ears now pricked I heard laughter and it was, without a shadow of a doubt, Max. "It can only be Max," I thought. "Apart from myself there is only one person I know who would prefer the meadows to the swimming pool on a day like this". I knew all the characters in the meadows. Besides, Max had a lifelong obsession with guns. "Max!" I shouted at the top of my voice. "Hi!" and "bang, bang, bang!" came the reply promptly. Despite the heat and the three-quarter-mile walk to the next fordable place, I decided to enquire. It wasn't difficult to find Max on the other side; the reports guided me to him.

Now, what he was doing there was most unusual: there he was, stretched flat out on his belly, gun in hand, aiming at the chub. On hot and sunny days in summer, chub bask in the sunshine just beneath the surface, so Max for some unfathomable reason decided to have a go at them with his gun. This was a highly bizarre scene, to say the least. "Bang, bang, bang!" the gun went and the chub dived; then, after a while, they rose again, settling in, and shortly afterwards they were shot at again. He missed all the time but that apparently didn't annoy him and he carried on shooting until he ran out of cartridges. The reason for missing the chub was the refraction of light and the state Max was in. Judging by his stubble, he had "worked a nightshift", meaning he had been drinking all night, not in the pub but out there in the meadows. For Max, the meadows in summer were something of an extension of home (wherever that was): an outdoor living room with nature as his television. "Why did you do that?" I asked him when he had finished the last round. He didn't give me an answer: he just laughed.

That laughter: it wasn't madness: mad, insane laughter has an edge to it you immediately recognise even if you have never heard it before. Max's laughter was a gentle chuckle with an occasional eruption into a loud "hah, hah". It came from deep, deep down and from way back in the past. Nothing primitive, more archaic in an educated way like perhaps a Celt would laugh. A Celt? Now that is highly romantic but then he did have pride, courage, refinement and a bold defiance, all the qualities ascribed to those Celtic warriors fighting naked against the Roman soldiers. There was something of the naked warrior in shooting at those chub. Beyond character, Max had a sort of inner link, a plug-in, to nature which made him the outstanding fisherman he was. He simply knew how, when, where and why to try for perch, pike, trout and carp. How he knew and where he had learned it, I don't know. Eager but less gifted fisherman like myself learn to look for tell-tale signs but never know in the sense that a fisherman like Max knows. Max's knowledge was aesthetic in the true sense of the word: sensory cognition. In practical terms this meant that he could be sleeping under a tree and simply wake up at the right time as if he had some inner alarm clock going off whenever the conditions were right for what he wanted to catch. The hard fact was: he consistently caught fish when others didn't, and if others caught fish, he caught more. Simple fact. Simple? He clearly perceived something we couldn't.

You probably intuitively realise that shooting chub is ugly. But why fuss over "frightening" a few chub and a bit of noise and water pollution (the bullets). No harm done, was there? Well, as a matter of fact there was: " a bit of noise and water pollution" is a bit too much because from the point of view of principle it doesn't matter whether the pollution is infinitesimal or gigantic. If it can be avoided, it ought to be avoided and while a non-angler might be excused on ignorance, there is no excuse for the angler. Celt or no Celt, shooting at chub is simply wrong. Let alone illegal possession of firearms, the complete absence of a sporting element and the utter pointlessness of it all.

Max forgot that the recreational angler, the sportsman, is *ipso facto* bound by a multitude of obligations which he must honour. One of those obligations is surely not to shoot at chub. Honour, by the way, is a concept that has largely gone out of fashion under the pressure of legal machineries endlessly producing laws and rights in the strange belief that quantity replaces quality – what used to be handshake is now a 500,000-word document. Even if for some strange reason shooting chub were legal, it still would be wrong and wouldn't belong to the beauty of angling.

The beauty of angling does not include the obviously ugly like discarding line, littering, deliberate foul-hooking, throwing hand grenades in pools, mindlessly and blindly stomping along the river bank or the moor squashing toads and birds' nests, putting back fish by hurling them through the air, cutting the drift of another boat and a thousand other things all of which you know are wrong when you see them. Most fishermen see when something is wrong; some don't see it at all and thus perform ugly acts like smashing beer bottles on a beach where they've had their picnic. You might say this is not half as bad because glass is not toxic and decomposes. That may be so, but by smashing bottles on a beach you aesthetically spoil the place for others, and glass cuts aren't exactly a pleasure either. Besides the act of smashing them has something akin to despicable wanton violence in it. Anglers and other people who commit ugly acts like that have an underdeveloped sense of beauty or duty. Anglers who do not see the obvious ugliness (wrongness) of their acts – for example, stealing fish by exceeding the bag limit and hoping to get away with it – can be taught. I think **one can learn about beauty just as one can learn about right and wrong,** good and bad, not least because there is beauty and ugliness, right and wrong, good and bad.

In order to leave ugliness behind us, I have to draw your attention to a vital distinction: while the ugly in fishing is positively and objectively wrong, there is absolutely nothing wrong with different styles and attitudes to fishing as long as they're in keeping with the general rules governing the fishing where you fish. There is nothing wrong, for example, with listening to techno beats with your Walkman while you fish. In my view, it is just bad style and a wasted opportunity because you probably miss out on almost everything that's going on around you. But it's not ugly. Likewise, there are attitudes I don't share, for example, excessive competitiveness. If you fish in the same boat with somebody who is obsessed by quantity, the emanating tenseness is so palpable, it spoils the atmosphere for me. Again, it is not ugly: there's nothing wrong with competitiveness as such. Fishermen can differ widely in style and attitude but as long as they're within the framework provided by the rules, that's perfectly okay. Like in almost all walks of life, however, there are borderline cases and who is to judge on attitude? Mrs. Aldridge is.

You have probably never heard of Mrs. Constance Aldridge of Mount Falcon Castle, Ballina, Ireland, who died in May 2003. God rest her soul. After the death of her husband in 1976, she restored

94

and ran the Castle as a guesthouse and it quickly turned into a Mecca for anglers. Mrs. Aldridge was an exceptional lady, greatly loved and respected by anglers from all over the world. A woman of great character, culture and authority, inspiring and running a house full of fun and laughter. The castle held some fishing rights on the famous Moy and was strategically placed for other fisheries up and downstream.

When I visited Mount Falcon Castle in the 1990s, its private beats were all booked. I got some fishing at Foxford, but not being an experienced salmon angler, made a fool of myself by fishing with a single-handed trout rod and the wrong flies and by stupidly losing a 14-pound salmon while trying to net it. To this very day I could slap myself for being such an ass. I had played and tired the salmon perfectly for a good half hour. I had him over my trout net, which was deep enough, but not quite wide enough. This normally wouldn't be a problem: you keep the line tight, get the fish dead centre over the net and then gently lift the net so that the salmon "folds" into it. In my excitement and temporary brain shutdown I slackened the line and jerked the net up. By doing so I lifted the salmon on the metal-rim of the net. All it had to do was to give one mighty lash with its tail and a vigorous shaking of the head to get rid of the hook which is just what it did. That was bad fishing, bad style, bad attitude and excessively stupid, but it was not ugly.

There were about a dozen anglers on that stretch of the Moy, but nobody felt crowded. Everybody was fly-fishing (the rule was "fly only") except for one German angler who was worming and shrimping with the head ghillie. The story behind that is told in one word: money. The fishing-right holder simply couldn't resist the offer that was made by the "angler". The sums that were bandied about sounded incredible but plausible, considering that our man was there for the whole season (apparently he had been coming for many years). Although I can empathise with the owner of the fishery to a degree, I don't understand the "angler" whom I once met in a pub. Beyond booze, boobs and brag, there was nothing in him. I am by no means objecting to the worming or shrimping as such (they should nevertheless be banned in salmon fishing), but what's the use of rules if you can simply buy your way out of them? I personally don't think this is a borderline case: it's ugly. What do you think?

Before I continue, I have to emphasise that I am not germanophobic; it's coincidence that the two "anglers" I am about to mention are also German. It isn't really germane to the topic whether they're German or not – they could be Swiss, French, Spanish, Italian. You find the type everywhere. The younger one was between 30 and 40, and the older probably around 55. Both looked impeccably spruce, boasting superb Swiss watches of the £10,000 class and a smashing BMW many times that amount. The two of them, I learned from their conversations in the salon and at the large dinner table at Mount Falcon, ran a highly successful tool-making firm. In their line they were probably the leading company, and their competence in that field of business was doubtless beyond question. The older man was the founder of the company and the younger man – not his son – the chosen successor. The latter knew about fishing. He had been salmon fishing in Norway, Canada and Scotland. The older man had apparently never fished before but for some strange reason was obsessed with the idea of catching a specimen salmon. Did he perhaps want to impress on the younger man that he could do anything, if only he put his mind to it?

Already the first evening when they came back from the river, you could detect an itching impatience in the older man: he moaned about the difficulty of casting and that they hadn't seen a fish. Wo sind die Lachse (Where are the salmon)? There was no need to understand German: the undertone in the question suggested the personal responsibility of Mrs. Aldridge for the apparent absence of salmon, and there was an unbearable haughtiness in it which made all those present inwardly groan. Mrs. Aldridge, who always presided over the dinner table took it with equanimity and gently steered the conversation away from fishing. In this she was helped by a German doctor who had been a regular visitor to Mount Falcon for a number of years. He was going to play an important role as an interpreter in the events that followed. Nobody had caught a salmon that day.

The second evening, our two teutons entered the salon where apéritifs were being served. The younger man greeted those present with a nervous, stiff smile and forced joviality. The boss sported a bilious stare signalling trouble. Seeing this, the German doctor tried to be friendly and managed to draw the two into a conversation during which the older man bitterly complained about not having caught a fish, pointing out twice that that was the sole purpose of his visit and what he had paid for. The situation was further aggravated in that he had discovered some illicit activity on the other bank. "Two poachers," the young man explained. "Poachers, poachers," the older parroted in a scandalised high pitch, making everybody in the salon look around. This prompted Mrs. Aldridge, who was talking to another guest, to join the German group to politely enquire whether there was any problem. The German doctor translated Mrs. Aldridge's question, whereupon a storm of condescending complaint showered on Mrs. Aldridge. As before, no need to understand German: the tone said it all. The German doctor desperately tried to soften the impact by giving Mrs. Aldridge a polite version of what effectively amounted to a sustained insult. **He wasn't paying, he said, for not catching salmon,** the potholes in the road and the insufficient parking at the riverside. He threw in a thousand and one other complaints in and around Mount Falcon. Mrs. Aldridge bore it with royal patience and luckily the general embarrassment was defused by the announcement that dinner would be served. Dinner passed in a slightly subdued mood with the doctor, now volunteering as a buffer, taking the brunt of the arrogant verbiage.

On the third evening, our friends didn't show in the salon for the apéritif but instead joined the other guests at the dinner table. A white-faced crown prince and a tyrant with a black expression forebode a storm which broke loose after the first course. Again, the man thought he had spotted poachers, again he hadn't caught a fish (nobody had) and again he let loose a volley of thinly disguised insults. The doctor didn't even bother to translate but pleaded with the man to stop. To no avail. At that point Mrs. Aldridge stood up and looked the man straight in the eye, and her posture and expression left little doubt that she meant business – serious business. There was something charismatic about her that simply commanded respect. The man shut up. "Out!" she simply said in a matter-of-fact voice and for emphasis she pointed to the door. "Leave my house immediately!" and after a little pause she added almost whispering, "I don't ever want to see you again – out, now!"

You could have heard a pin drop in the dinning room. As if hypnotised or under a spell, the two silently and meekly left the

room and went packing. Chance had it that the moment they came down the stairs, the dining room door was opened by the service staff, and the guests (Mrs. Aldridge sat with her back to the door) could see the two banned anglers heaving their heavy luggage down the stairs. The older one had regained his speech and could be heard swearing and cursing. Shortly afterwards, the engine of the BMW gave a mighty roar and the wheels spun in the gravel.

Then dead silence followed by loud, liberating laughter around the table. Mrs. Aldridge didn't join in and when everybody had recovered, conversation resumed. The incident wasn't mentioned by anybody: like a nightmare once over, you didn't really want to dissect it. No need to – you know it's ugly. Their whole attitude was wrong (bad, ugly) from the start. Trophy hunting is not bad as such, not at all, but expecting to be successful because you assume everything can be bought is not just unreal but – again – ugly. The next day Mrs. Aldridge and her guests were in the best of spirits: salmon had been caught left, right and centre.

Ah, the beauty of it...

The Assistant Bailiff's Brother's Fly

Kitsch either means "artistic vulgarity: sentimentality, tastelessness, or ostentation in any of the arts" or "vulgar objects: collectively, decorative items that are regarded as tasteless, sentimental or ostentatious in style" (Microsoft Encarta Dictionary). There is often a note of condescension in its use. The user, by the very definition of the word, is making a value judgement. Note the difference between saying, "this is kitsch" and "I don't like this". By using "kitsch" there is a pretence at objectivity. The user can hide behind some convenient cloud-cuckoo-land standard and avoid any commitment.

Tackle shops are places of pilgrimage and according to the above definition, full of kitsch. Just think of those little porcelain statues portraying either angler or fish or both. Or the decorated knives and flasks; or watches with fish motifs; or T-Shirts; or ties with trout on them – there are thousands and thousands of objects qualifying as kitsch and in my view this is part of the beauty of angling. You see, the problem with kitsch resides in "that are regarded as...". Who is the anonymous authority judging and, more often than not, deriding the sentiments (emotions, feelings) of pilgrims and anglers (and a lot of other people who are not pilgrims and anglers)? Well, I think, there is a thing like *Zeitgeist* (spirit of the age) which tries to dictate the mores in all areas of life. The producers and executioners of the *Zeitgeist* are a multitude of persons in universities, schools, the media, political parties and other institutions all disseminating more or less the same ideas – the political correctness posse.

Sentiment as in, for example, Landseer's (Sir Edwin Landseer, 1802–1873) "The Old Shepherd's Chief Mourner" (the picture shows a dog putting its head on the shepherd's coffin) is practically universally

derided as kitsch by the *Zeitgeist* gurus. In like manner displays of devotional objects are often ridiculed – that is, if they're Christian; if they're not Christian you'll have to respect and appreciate them as great manifestations of a foreign culture. I think there's a priori nothing wrong with sentiment and sentimental displays. Wouldn't it make scores of psychologists jobless if there were more kitsch in the world? Be that as it may, I for one try to avoid the word "kitsch": I dislike its pseudo- elitist convenience.

Nature isn't tied to the *Zeitgeist* or specific concepts of kitsch and beauty. In order to participate in the beauty of nature, you don't need to go angling. There are many sports and pursuits like birdwatching, walking, windsurfing and golfing which take place in nature's arena. The big difference between all those and angling is the degree of involvement. Angling draws you deeper into the works, so to speak, than following the fairways or any other nature-related sports which only scratch the surface. Angling more than any other pursuit has and always had an inquisitive, contemplative and meditative side to it. On which other "pastime" converge such a multitude of diverse elements? Besides, do you know of any pursuit which regularly surprises and delights with the unexpected, mysterious and hilarious?

If, for example, you breed your own worms, you'll have to delve into composting, show an interest in dung and dung heaps and acquaint yourself with the different species of worms. There is no fish as good as the one you caught with your self-bred worm or self-tied fly or self-mixed boilies. Bait which I have only mentioned in passing when talking about the triad of hook, knot and line is, of course, just as important as all the other factors in the basic angling equation.

Although it is true, for example, that perch will sometimes go for an empty shining hook, this isn't the rule. Fishing is about seduction and the fundamental law of all kinds of professional seduction is that the bait must be attractive to the fish and not to the angler (there are more anglers than fish who are seduced by flies). This fundamental law presupposes, of course, that there are fish to catch. In other words if you want to catch fish, make sure you fish where there are fish.

The most vexing problem in my early boyhood fishing years was to understand that fish were not where I would have liked them to be. Also, they didn't behave as I wished they would behave. I fished at the times which seemed right to me and at the places which seemed right to me and with the bait that seemed right to me. This was no more than daydreaming with a rod at the riverside. No wonder I was more often than not terribly disappointed but eventually it dawned on me that fishing reality was different from what I had supposed.

Years later the process was repeated when I started fly-fishing. Although I was fully aware of the basic entomological facts, I systematically ignored them in my first season and put on what I fancied. I was seduced by the flies and caught, of course, only the odd fish. Once I started to observe, to analyse, to reason and to proceed systematically, I started catching fish regularly. But back to the quintessential point about the bait needing to be attractive to the fish and not to the angler.

The other day I was fishing the Schoolhouse Loch (Loch Culag) at Lochinver. At least through the eye of the fisherman the school there probably qualifies as one of the world's most interestingly and beautifully situated schoolhouses. Even though the village of Lochinver is nearby and the schoolhouse is easily accessible, it looks sometimes a little bit lost and lonely on its little spit of land. The loch itself is small, separated from the sea only by the short and cascading River Culag. I had been fishing there all morning in bright sunshine and there wasn't even the hint of a breeze.

As I pulled in for lunch I saw a man sitting by the mooring. He helped me secure the boat, and from the way he tied the knot I could tell he was no stranger to boats. He was a strong fellow of about thirty and introduced himself as the bailiff's assistant. Our conversation turned first to fishing in general then to his job, my job, the economy, back to fishing, to God and the world. What agreeable company! Time flew.

As we were about to say goodbye, he rummaged about in his pockets and finally extracted a little fly box. He opened it, picked a fly, handed it to me and said, "if nothing catches this will". I looked at the fly. It was the most untidy fly I'd ever seen. No proportions, no skill required to tie it. The assistant bailiff must have seen the shadows of doubt passing my face. He explained that he himself had had doubts when his brother had given him this fly to try. Success, however, had convinced him. "It will catch, don't worry," he reassured me.

I put the epitome of lousy fly-tying in my box and started the afternoon's proceedings with my reliable old guard, i.e. Black, Pennel on the tail, Wickham's Fancy on the dropper and Bibio on the bob. Conditions didn't improve; I changed flies to no avail. I didn't stir a fin. Inwardly I had almost resigned myself to a blank when I decided to give The Assistant Bailiff's Brother's Fly a go. After all, it couldn't do worse than any of the previously tried patterns.

I put it on the bob and would you believe it? Hardly ten minutes passed before the first violent take by a trout. Conditions hadn't changed one bit – it was still bright, sunny and not a hint of wind. Amazing. I was positively baffled at the end of the day with a fine brace of small brown trout and a two-pound sea trout thrown in for good measure. Back at the hotel I learned that nobody else had caught anything, which made me decide to keep quiet about my secret weapon. I have done so ever since because The Assistant Bailiff's Brother's Fly (TABBF) has consistently caught me brown trout and sea trout (no salmon... yet).

I think it was Kenichiro Sawada, the Japanese master fly-tier, who said something like,

"it is our aim to catch beautiful trout with beautiful flies"

What a remarkable maxim and on the face of it the antithesis to the dictum of the bait having to be attractive to the fish and not to the fisherman. Certainly not every beautiful fly is attractive to trout. There is, however, no reason why beauty should exclude attractiveness. Ken Sawada's flies and the way he portrays them are stunningly beautiful. There is perfection in craft, proportion, colour and a powerful self-evidence about them which makes you physically feel the chasm between what is a worthy fly and your own poor hackle on the hook. It most certainly isn't Sawada's aim

110

to discourage fly-tiers by his own perfection. Quite the contrary: by his example he shows what beauty is possible and by trying to tie your flies beautifully or to make them beautiful and catching, you advance in your fishing.

What about the scruffy TABBF? To trout it most certainly looks extremely attractive, i.e. mouth-watering, so to speak. What the TABBF lacks in craft, proportion and clarity it makes up for in efficiency. Do I, by using the TABBF, disqualify from "beautiful fishing"? I don't think so, because the basic goal of fishing is to catch fish with sporting methods. Certainly my TABBF qualifies there and everything on a higher level than the TABBF is a refinement which adds more pleasure. So if I am not content to catch trout the ordinary TABBF way, I can try to intensify my pleasure by refinement in method, such as by tying beautiful flies. Either way I add to the beauty and culture of angling.

THE MARMORATA QUARTET

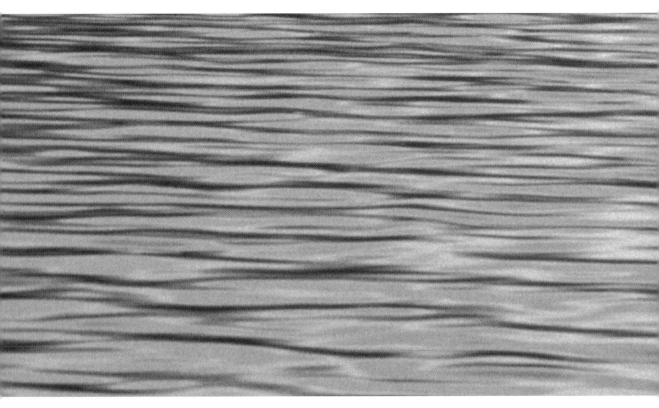

And now for the water, the element I trade in. The water is the eldest daughter of the creation, the element upon which the Spirit of God did first move, the element which God commanded to bring forth living creatures abundantly... [water] is the chief ingredient in the creation: many philosophers have made it to comprehend all the other elements, and most allow it the chiefest in the mixtion of all living creatures.

Izaac Walton, 1653

113

This is Walton on water in 1653 and he points to the obvious so that it doesn't get overlooked: the miracle of life. Modern science bears out Walton's assumption about water being "the chiefest in the mixtion of all living creatures". The most watery of all creatures is the freshwater jellyfish which consists of 99.3% of water. In comparison human beings are relatively dry, with up to 70% water; and 70% of the earth's surface is covered with water in one form or another. 97% of all water is salt water. Very little of the remaining 3% is in free circulation and fishable.

The worlds of Ted Leeson, Viktor Schauberger and Ted Hughes are as far apart as can be, but water unites them in interest. In his *Jerusalem Creek* the American writer Ted Leeson composed a chapter on meandering, from which the following passage is taken.

A meandering stream takes the shape it must, conforming to the principles of dynamics and work and energy balance. But as in other forms that shape themselves around other constraints – the hexagon of snowflakes or the helix of DNA, a sonnet or the blues – the borders still afford ample room for variety and distinctiveness. A few basic ratios of arithmetic can give rise to the most elegant representations. A spring creek meanders through shapely permutations, through close, backtracking turns that nearly touch one another; in regular, rhythmic alternations, clean as a sine wave; around right angle corners; along flexing arcs that wobble as they bend; and through the graceful, elongated S-curves that are perhaps the loveliest of all. The eighteenth-century painter William Hogarth called this curve "the line of beauty" and pronounced it the most aesthetically perfect of all shapes. It is a line of both motion and repose, a figure repeated in the dip and swell of rolling hills, the swerve of schooling fish, the twist of a vine through the understory, the curve of a woman's back. In a painting, Hogarth said, this line of beauty "leads the eye on a wanton kind of chase." In nature, it leads the feet as well.

The meandering stream is an instance of a cosmic theme. The theme is life. Viktor Schauberger (1885–1958) a non-conformist, controversial thinker and inventor of the "trout turbine" takes the theme of life to its logical conclusion:

The upholder of the cycles which sustain all Life is water. In every drop of water dwells a deity whom indeed we all serve. There also dwells Life, the soul of the primal substance – water – whose boundaries and banks are the capillaries that guide it, and in which it circulates. Every pulse beat arising through the interaction of will and resistance is indicative of creative work and urges us to care for those vessels, those primary and most vital structures, in which throbs the product of a dualistic power – Life.

Every waterway is an artery of this Life, an artery that creates its own pathways and bridges as it advances, so as to diffuse its dawning life-force through the Earth and elevate itself to great heights, to become shining, beautiful and free. Standing at the highest level of evolution, and above all being blessed with mind and reason, humanity constantly does the most idiotic thing imaginable by trying to regulate these waterways by means of their banks – by influencing the flow mechanically, instead of taking into account the fact that water itself is a living entity.

The meandering stream not only reveals its own microstructure (spiral shapes, motions, vortices etc.) but also that of life itself in as much as it resembles remarkably the DNA structure (water is part of DNA). Such visual similarity might be purely coincidental but in his inspiring book *The Cosmic Serpent – DNA and the Origins of Knowledge*, Jeremy Narby shows that the opposite might well be the case. In a nutshell his story is that knowledge about life (DNA) was lying around everywhere and all you need to do is to try and pick it up as did and do all cultures at all times. Whether for Peruvian or Siberian tribes, in ancient Egypt or modern Europe, spiral shapes, often in the form of a serpent are the give-away clue. After discussing one of many spiral-shape instances and its attributes, the Egyptian cosmic serpent, Narby sums up:

What else could the Ancient Egyptians have meant when they talked of a double serpent, provider of attributes and key of life, if not what scientists call "DNA"?

Why are these metaphors so consistently and so frequently used unless they mean what they say?

A friend told me that she never saw so many pregnant women as when she herself was pregnant. The same goes for spiral shapes:

once you start looking for them you see them everywhere: snails, spiralling nebulae, waves, drills, logarithms, spouts, pine cones, ice creams, mountain roads, staircases, snake rings on the fly rod, line coils, flag pole decoration, bath-tub vortices, yin and yang, caduceus, falling leaves, ivy, corkscrews, brains and dances – whatever, life is the theme of water and after Leeson's composition, Schauberger's analysis, Narby's exploration and speculation, here is a deeply probing poem about life by Ted Hughes' the key passage of which refers, of course, to a spiral shape.

Salmon Eggs

The salmon were just down there –
Shuddering together, touching each other,
Emptying themselves for each other –

Now beneath flood-murmur
They curve deadwards.

                     January haze,
With a veined yolk of sun. In bone-damp cold
I lean and watch the water, listening to water
Till my eyes forget me

And the piled flow supplants me, the mud-blooms

All this ponderous light of everlasting
Collapsing away under its own weight

Mastodon ephemera

Mud-curdling, bull-dozing, hem-twinkling
Caesarian of heaven and earth, unfelt

With exhumations and delirious advents –

                         Catkins

Wriggle at their mother's abundance. The spider clings to his craft.

Something else is going on in the river

More vital than death – death here seems a superficiality
Of small scaly limbs, parasitical. More grave than life
Whose reflex jaws and famished crystals
Seem incidental
To this telling – these toilings of plasm –
The melt of mouthing silence, the charge of light
Dumb with immensity.

          The river goes on
Sliding through its place, undergoing itself
In its wheel.

          I make out the sunk foundations
Of burst crypts, a bedrock
Time-hewn, time-riven altar. And this is the liturgy
Of the earth's tidings – harrowing, crowned - a travail
Of raptures and rendings.

          Sanctus Sanctus

Swathes the blessed issue.

          Perpetual mass

Of the waters
Wells from the cleft.

          It is the swollen vent

Of the nameless
Teeming inside atoms – and inside the haze
And inside the sun and inside the earth.

It is the font, brimming with touch and whisper
Swaddling the egg.

          Only birth matters
Say the river's whorls.

          And the river
Silences everything in a leaf-mouldering hush
Where sun rolls bare, and earth rolls,

And mind condenses on old haws.

118

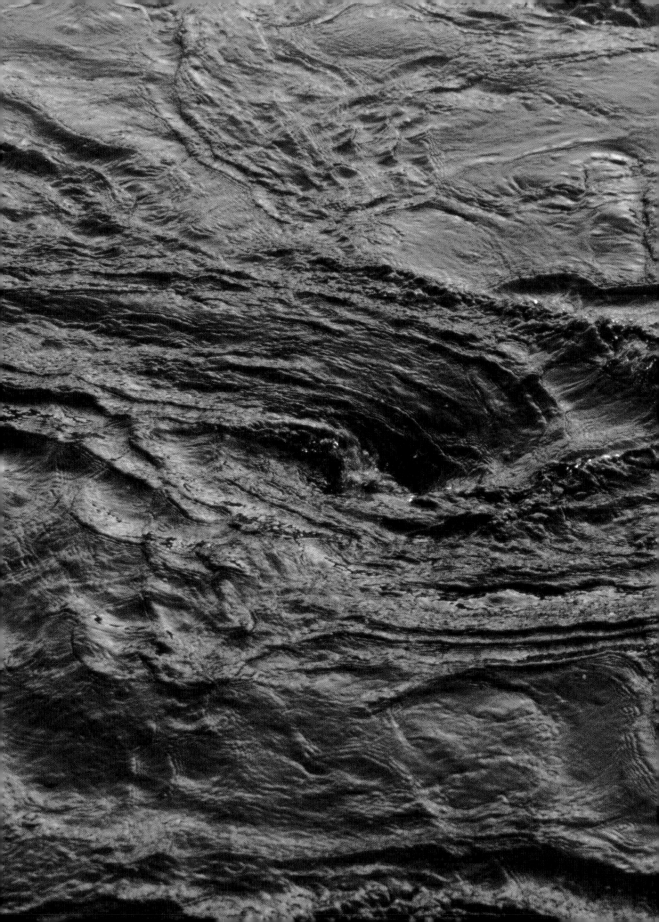

"The blood of the earth" (Schauberger) is the most beautiful and most essential stuff there is. No water, no fish – no water, no life. It's as simple as that. "Simple": there's that word again. Today the public at large is beginning to wake up to the fact that there is more to water than a dripping tap. The free and ready supply of water has made it for decades the most undervalued (in the non-pecuniary sense) commodity in the eyes of non-fishermen. Witness to this are the inordinate amounts of pure drinking water being used to flush toilets, to shave or to wash cars. A little pee flushed with six litres of pure drinking water is somehow out of proportion. Waste disposal (ground water), sewage treatment and air pollution (fall out) prevention are topics dear to the heart of every angler (have you ever been to a sewage treatment plant?). Pollution is an issue where even the most radical animal rightists, the most militant vegetarians and the most revolutionary environmentalists are in accord with anglers and hunters. They may be, philosophically and ideologically speaking, worlds apart but a polluted river or seashore is a disaster for all of us. Pollution is ugly, but not all that looks ugly is pollution.

Slaughterhouse waste used to be drained into rivers or lakes. A sight which didn't please too many people except, of course, the angler in the know. The vicinity of the slaughterhouse drain was the hot spot. Nowhere else would the trout be that big and that strong and that good. However, in some places here in Switzerland real pollution seemed to get completely out of hand in the Sixties and Seventies, and for once political action (not least due to the pressure and initiative of anglers) was swift and efficient. Today some lakes here have the problem of being too clean (enthusiasm confused clean and sterile) which is the reason why some species of fish in Swiss lakes are today smaller than they were 30 years ago. However, the problem has been recognised and I am optimistic that sooner or later a proper balance will be found again.

Estimates for the average amount of water used per person per day in Europe and the United States vary from country to country between 100 and 150 litres a day which are split up roughly as follows:

Shower / bath	26 %
Personal hygiene	8 %
Cooking / drinking	4 %
Dishwashing	12 %
Cleaning	5 %
Toilet	31 %
Laundry	14 %

The 100-litre usage in a village with a thousand people yields 36,500,000 litres which go down the drain per annum. Unbelievable isn't it? Now just think what a fantastic achievement it already is to treat and clean this used water charged with human waste and chemicals of all sorts. It will be rightly pointed out that certain chemicals (e.g. tensides) and hormones still find a way through the "filters" and combine to bad effects (e.g. infertile fish). Add to this industrial and agricultural waste and you suddenly begin to understand what incredible pressure we put on our water which after all – it can't be emphasised enough – is the basis of life and fishing. Yet again I am confident that solutions will be found if there is a political will for it (brought about by lobbying from anglers). There's also another source for this optimism: a lot of know-how has been obtained in recent decades and there is definitely business to be done in water treatment, water saving and water distribution. There are for example market-ready systems which collect rainwater from the roof. The water is used then for the toilets, the laundry, the car and the garden. The return of the allis shad and salmon to the Rhine is living proof of the progress that water-treatment has made.

Richard Louv, author of that great book on American angling *Fly-Fishing for Sharks*, suggests that if you run into an anti-angler you should ask him "How many rivers have you saved lately?" I think this is brilliant because it makes a positive statement about anglers while putting the antis on the spot. It has often been pointed out that anglers are the guardians of our waters. Probably eight out of ten pollution incidents are first spotted and reported by anglers. Anglers are also the first to notice fish disease and other longer-term changes in the water environment, such as increase in algae growth. The point is that this responsiveness and the subsequent cleaning and the restoration of water habitats get very little attention if they aren't sold properly. Let me illustrate this. Just a week ago we had a case of chloride spillage from a swimming pool, killing literally thousands of trout. The headline in the newspaper read, "Pollution kills thousands of trout!" I don't think in three or five years' time when life has come back to that stream, there will be a headline: "Anglers' success: trout are back!" Nobody will notice or know – except the anglers of course.

The anglers' commitment to nature tends to be simply forgotten or ignored, partly because the antis succeed in portraying anglers as greedy fish murderers, partly because there is nothing spectacular about fish as such (most of the time they can't even be seen) and partly because some anglers are hesitant to communicate. They love to show off their specimen fish but keep strangely quiet about their real achievements. Add to this that not many people in the public at large understand what it means to resuscitate a stream (a river, a lake) and you understand why the anglers' achievement isn't clearly discernible. Initiating, participating and watching over environmental schemes in and around aquatic environments is part of every angler's business and the angling fraternity (and sisterhood, of course) shouldn't hide its light under a bushel. On the contrary: false modesty is detrimental to the angling interest which is best served by active communication in general and by securing political influence. In other words, anglers have to learn from their enemies. "Active communication" means that in five years' time when the trout are back in that little stream, anglers must make an effort to get into the headlines with "Anglers' success: trout are back!"

Most people react positively on seeing a stream or a river (for real or in a picture) meandering through the meadows. In fact, most waterscapes please and will meet with aesthetic approval and be termed as "beautiful". There is something beyond utility, everybody instantly recognises. Waterscapes are the perfect instances where the good and the beautiful meet and where they are obviously the two sides of the same coin. What could be more of a good than water and life?

"Most waterscapes please" I said above. The exceptions are, of course, polluted waterscapes or threatening waterscapes like pictures of huge, gloomy, leaden waves rolling towards the observer.

Equally intimidating is a hurricane-whipped sea crashing violently against the shore. Yet in the end even in such pictures of unleashed force attraction holds sway over fear. For one thing, it's a picture one is looking at. This is fairly safe but people with a lively imagination immediately see stories and dangers in such pictures – the ship in the storm, the rambler in peril on the cliff, the breaking dike, the unsuspecting angler wading in a stream about to be swept away by a flood and so on. Nevertheless, even when confronted with real waves in a real world with real dangers, you can't help feeling that there is something beautiful about the elemental force of water. On the opposite end in terms of size are Masaru Emoto's pictures of water crystals. These are waterscapes at a microscopic level, and while I am not convinced by the theories behind those water crystals I admire their beauty. I also like the idea that even on a microscopic level "good water looks good" and "bad water looks bad". The stream meandering through the meadows looks good and is good when certain indicators (like fish, like insect life, like flora and fauna) are present. It doesn't look good if these are absent. To the trained eye, that is – if you don't know what a healthy stream looks like, you could be deceived by appearance.

There's nothing as boring as a blue sky (besides, most of the time it's no good for fishing); a sky alive with drifting clouds is one of the most beautiful shows there is, and looking for faces and animals in clouds is not only highly entertaining but free. The most rewarding thing in cloud watching is, however, simply enjoying the beauty of it. Immersing yourself in the sky, so to speak, because **by looking at clouds you're looking at water.** Cloudscapes are waterscapes. Imagine now the following picture: you see a lake and right down to the shore, the woods; above the woods the still snow-capped peaks and yet above them a cloud-laden sky. If there is a little rain at the same time then you're almost completely enveloped in water. That which is not entirely water (you, the plants, the trees, the land) is very watery nevertheless (remember, you're 70% water) or involved in the water cycle. So to call scenery such as I have just described a landscape would be a first-class misnomer. Most landscape painting (except desert themes) depicts water in one form or another. This reminds me of a second misnaming: the sunset. The sun never sets or rises. What happens is that the sun is simply there and that the Earth orbits around it and rotates around its own axis.

When a part of the Earth moves out of the direct light of the sun, it's a "sunset" there. The sunset in reality is an earthset. Poets, scientists and most people fully aware of the fact will, however, use "sunset" instead of "earthset". The word sunset better captures the spirit of the event, which is why in the end sunset is the right word. The sun is at the centre of the water cycle. It supplies the energy for the process. Most of the environment is in one way or another involved in the water cycle, which is why when you take an interest in water you take an interest in the world itself, in life itself, in beauty itself. This distinguishes fishing from common sports – you don't have to know about the water cycle to win the World Cup in any sport, but you need to know about water and the water cycle if you want to be a good and successful fisherman.

It might be objected that you can enjoy the miracles and gifts of nature without being a fisherman. Of course, if you go on walks you get involved in the many questions and curiosities of nature. Walking or rambling, exploring the countryside, surely is the next best thing to fishing because it provokes many of the same questions as fishing does. Landscape painting or nature and underwater photography certainly also guide you to the discovery of our world's beauty. But the more specialised the pursuit becomes, the more the angle of contemplation and practical knowledge narrows. Let me illustrate this. Kayaking is no doubt a great pastime and the great crested grebe is a great bird. Where's the link?

The other day I was fishing on Lake Thun. Since early spring I had been watching a pair of great crested grebes. Their courtship display has to be seen to be believed – this is a ritual of great elaboration and elegance. I like these birds because they're a pleasure to look at and somehow give the impression of being extremely quick-witted. Lake Thun isn't the easiest of environments for them to breed in. The lake can get unbelievably busy at peak times in late spring and early summer. Nevertheless, the pair succeeded in raising one chick. This particular day was on a hot weekend and the lake was extremely busy. I was fishing at a fairly secluded spot and also watching the grebes. The male was busy diving for small fish while the mother and the one (remaining?) chick waited for him about ten yards from the shore. Whenever a craft came too close for comfort the mother would quickly hide under some overhanging tree roots. A leisurely and silently approaching kayaker took her by surprise and she panicked, letting herself be driven by the zigzagging kayaker for about fifty yards. The kayaker was absolutely unaware that he was driving a panicking bird and her offspring just in front of him. I shouted and waved to no avail: the reckless kayaker just didn't take any notice. He wasn't aware of anything. Luckily, he decided to change course and the grebe made it back to base. What I am accusing here is not kayaking, but the thoughtless kayaker. Disturbing nesting birds by accident can happen – disturbing nesting birds by negligence doesn't happen to a good fisherman.. By trying to catch fish, the fisherman becomes more alert, more involved and at the same time more detached than, say, the walker, the surfer or the kayaker. More involved means the fisherman has a vital interest in what happens in the freshwater universe – also that which to other people is invisible or not important. Being more alert means the fisherman has a vital interest in seeing what is going on around him and to act accordingly. Being more detached means the fisherman has a vital interest in discovering connections and truth. All of this combined with the practical knowledge of fishing makes angling a unique pastime – no other recreational activity or sport involves such a range.

Is angling a pastime? Given its all-embracing ramifications, scope and reach, it is clearly not. It is a state of mind, a way of living, a state of being. The real angler is an angler at all times. This doesn't mean he is constantly thinking about fishing but that his attitude to life in general is that of the angler. The virtues of angling are the virtues of "ordinary life"; the angler doesn't change character or personality when not angling. Or to put it the other way round, no personality change occurs when one goes fishing. It is true, though, that some people really think there are two lives, i.e. angling and not angling, the latter being good the former bad. Nothing could be more of a self-delusion. Angling and not angling are two different states but never two different lives.

The confusion originates in the "get-away-from-it-all" myth, which is probably as old as fishing itself. If a fisherman comes back with a catch he is of course happy and relaxed – nothing is more self-evident. In order to catch those fish, the fisherman had literally

127

to get away from it all (to the right river or stream, at the right spot, at the right time etc.); he had to separate himself from his usual environment. When he sets out, he might still be caught up with everyday worries; when he gets back he is happy. No wonder people have thus associated getting away from everyday life and coming back with fish as relaxing. In recent decades, the "get-away-from-it-all" idea has been cast in iron by marketing and advertising to the degree that life only happens when you're away from it all. Nothing could be further from the truth – wherever you go, whatever you do you always take yourself with you. What happens in fact is the reverse of what is being claimed. **When going fishing you don't get away from it all, you come to terms with it all.** "It" here means basically yourself, your world and the world at large, which is why you don't change to a different life when fishing but simply change a state. Angling is not a pastime but a state of being, which means you are what you are when you don't fish and you are what you are when you do. There is no way to get away from it all!

The slightly different emphasis in the following lines by A.J. McClane perfectly complement the above:

Psychologists tell us that one reason we enjoy fishing is because it is an escape. This is meaningless. True, a man who works in the city wants to "escape" to the country, but the clinical implication is that (no matter where a man lives), he seeks to avoid reality. This is as obtuse as the philosophical doctrine which holds that no reality exists outside the mind.

Perhaps it's the farm boy in me, but I would apply Aristotelian logic - the chicken came before the egg because it is real and the egg is only potential. By the same reasoning the fluid content of a stream is nothing but water when it erupts from a city faucet, but given shores it becomes a river, and as a river it is perfectly capable of creating life, and therefore it is real. It is not a sewer, nor a conveyor of barges and lumber, although it can be pressed to those burdens and, indeed, as a living thing it can also be lost in its responsibilities.

So if escapism is a reason for angling – then the escape is to reality. (*Fisherman's Bounty*)

A couple of years back we headed for Slovenia. "We" were my non-fishing friend Peter and myself. The plan called for Peter to walk and for me to fish the world-famous Soca for a week. Our hotel was in the village of Kobarid. I never got a chance to fish the Soca because of rain upstream, it was fairly murky. Fishable, but after exploring the alternatives, I decided to spend my time at that fascinating tributary the Idrijca instead, as it wasn't affected by the rain.

Touring the region you can't help noticing the numerous war memorials and war cemeteries. These bear witness to World War I when the Soca valley and region saw the worst of the worst of that most brutal of all wars. You might have heard or read about Verdun on the Western front but what happened in the Julian Alps, at the Isonzo (Isonzo is the Italian name for the Soca) front, is simply beyond imagination in terms of atrocity, inhumanity, misery and suffering. Young Ernest Hemingway was the American war correspondent in the region where hundreds and hundreds of thousands of soldiers and civilians lost their lives in a theatre of stunning beauty. Not far behind in brutality and deceit were the Highland Clearances in Scotland, which are after all the reason why the Highlands can be advertised as Europe's last unspoiled countryside... or let Irish history pass before your mind's eye. Why make a point of what is the antithesis to the peace and harmony of angling? Angling is not escapism and while it is certainly not necessary to be interested in the history of the places you fish, it doesn't do any harm either to know about it. Knowledge of the non-fishing kind about where you are will not make you catch more fish. On the contrary, a visit to a museum or a site of interest might lose you fishing time during which there could have been the most fantastic rise – but then again you could think about all this in terms of a tangle. **I think knowing about the place you fish adds spice to the enjoyment and experience.**

This, you might object, is the approach of an old man who has caught many fish and can afford to be at ease. The average punter wants to catch fish, big fish and many fish and that is exactly what the angling travel business promises. Look at any brochure trying to sell dream fishing holidays. First and foremost fish are shown – rightly so because it's about fishing and who, myself included, wouldn't like to catch a big salmon or a huge pike? All the brochures

clearly suggest that could be you, that you'll catch such a whopper. There's nothing wrong with that either, because being full of happy anticipation is a pleasant experience. There is, however, a thin line between happy (and realistic) anticipation and hyped-up fish-catching fantasies fuelled by not only the travel agencies and fishing media, but also by fishing friends. Expectations and self-imposed pressures are sky-high.

With us in the hotel at Kobarid were four young French anglers between twenty and thirty years old. They always moved around in a group, they always smoked and it didn't cross their minds that there might be somebody outside France who understood French. They didn't feel in any way restrained in the use of their voices, so they unintentionally entertained us from two tables away with their conversation and remarks about the food and the wine at the hotel.

The first evening they discussed their plans for the following five days. They had set their minds to catching a marmorata, a marble trout. The marble trout is an exceedingly beautiful fish, endemic in that region and very, very difficult to catch on the fly. Nevertheless, they were glowing with enthusiasm and their systematic approach would have honoured a space mission. Among other paraphernalia they had maps with them, thermometers, diving masks and mobile phones. From amidst the clouds of smoke and an atmosphere of busy enervation, Peter and I gathered that they planned to fish for the marble trout in the Soca. I thought this very odd: the Soca was still very coloured while the Idrijca, where there are also marmorata, was in perfect condition. The four Frenchmen's comments on the food were, as you would expect, very knowledgeable and very favourable, full of praise, and they didn't find fault with the Slovenian wine either. Five days later, on the last evening, the food was lousy the wine diabolical and practically everything was labelled *moche*. Nothing was *moche*, of course. The food, the wine and the service were as outstanding as they had been on the first day. If anything the chef had surpassed himself during the week. He had in fact prepared trout in various ways – I distinctly remember a trout *carpaccio* which was out of this world. What had happened to the marmorata quartet?

Our friends certainly weren't beginners. They were early risers and excellent casters. I could see them now and then fishing the milky

Soca when I drove to my favourite haunt at the karstic Idrijca, where the water was as clear as slivovitz. This was near a little village called Slap where the *Gostlina Slap* restaurant served a cured ham which put any *prosciutto di Parma* to shame. This restaurant was above the Idrijca and you could sit there enjoying ham, bread and wine and a superb view on the Idrijca. Upstream of the restaurant there is a little road to the right leading down to a bridge over the Idrijca. Across the bridge is to the left and right a track along the river. From the bridge you look down on a pool at the tail of which runs a rocky plateau where you can cast upstream or across.

On my very first day crossing the bridge for the first time, I spotted downstream a snow-white Alfa Romeo parked off the footpath. I didn't really like the sight of it – that white, flashy car in a spring pasture full of wild flowers looked like a scene out of an advert for washing powder. Feeling that my preconceived ideas of beauty would get the better of me, I resolved to be open-minded about it. *A priori* I reminded myself there is nothing wrong with a big white Alfa Romeo amidst wild flowers. As the scene in question was just a couple of steps from the bridge, I reached it in no time; and long before I reached a conclusion about its aesthetic status. In the event my fears, prejudices, preconceived ideas, mental reservations and blockages started melting away rapidly.

As I approached the car I apprehended a movement, a gesture which I immediately understood: there was somebody in there tying a fly. It flashed across my mind that there is no sight like a white Alfa Romeo in wild grass provided a fly is being tied in there. Introductions were quickly made. Giovanni was from Udine, which is only a couple of hours' drive away. He and his son who fished further downstream had been coming to the Idrijca for donkey's years. Giovanni was Old School, a gentleman such as you don't meet too often these days. He was from a time when glove compartments actually contained gloves and not a complete fly-tying kit. The glove compartments of the Alfa had been converted into a mobile fly-tying unit. You could see from a mile that this was a professional job – it looked at first a bit incongruent in this mobile monument of Italian design and engineering. On the other hand the fly-tying unit was so cleverly integrated and so well-finished, I began to think that Alfa glove compartments are really meant for fly-tying units. Giovanni and I got along like a house on fire. He knew his fishing and his flies and happily volunteered all the information I needed for fishing that particular stretch of the Idrijca. Generously he also gave me a few flies, all of which proved to be veritable killers. We met every day for a chat in the white Alfa. I had great fishing at the Idrijca, catching a fair share of trout.

While I couldn't have been in better spirits, the mood of the smoky marmorata quartet deteriorated by the day. They were first out in the morning and last home in the evening – just in time for dinner. Once or twice they even missed it. The language they used among themselves reflected the growing strain. They began to scoff at each other's suggestions and their faces suggested dead serious, grim determination: we have a mission, we have a job to do, we are the pros, nothing will stand in our way, we'll get there whatever the cost. Fishing Rambos with the *idée fixe* that their marmorata would be waiting for them in the still slightly milky Soca. I don't know who had put it in their heads that marmorata could only be caught in the Soca and I don't know why suddenly only two days before their week ended they woke up to the fact that they could try the Tomlinka or the Idrijca. On the last day of their fishing I was chatting with Giovanni when the slamming of car doors startled us both and made us look towards the bridge: arrival of the smoky marmorata quartet. Cigarette in hand or in mouth or on its way to it, they looked over the parapet our way downstream. Much gesticulating, index fingers being pointed towards the water. Then a pow wow, a cloud of smoke hanging over the four heads. **Decision: car doors flung open, distribution of equipment.** With diving masks and thermometer they go to either end of the pool and look and measure. The pool underneath the bridge is a deep little gorge with whirlpools, eddies and undermined parts. Deep down there the specimen marmorata (and brown trout) wait for the night before they leave their hideouts in search of food. Big fish need lots of food: Giovanni recommends mouse, frog or toad imitations which, by the way, are perfectly in line with Izaak Walton's advice for catching big trout:

...and if there be a good trout in the hole he will take it, especially if the night be dark; for then he is bold, and lies near the top of the water, watching the motion of any frog, or water rat that swims between him and the sky..."

Anyway, the recce had apparently come to an end and as quickly and noisily as the marmorata quartet had appeared, they vanished again. Peace and quiet reigned. Late in the afternoon that day, they burst in once more and I happened to be again with Giovanni on my way back from the day's fishing. This time they were fully equipped and started fishing frantically. Two at the neck, two at the tail of the pool. What a strange sight that was: four lines being cast in a relatively small space. Despite the underlying hectic and the incessant smoking, they didn't tangle, which says something about their technical skills. I briefly explained the situation to Giovanni and hardly had the last word left my lips than a cry of relief made us look towards the bridge. There we saw one of the quartet obviously into a big fish. The bent rod looked as if it couldn't take much more and the angler played it carefully. His colleague was ready with the net in no time at all. And the others had, of course, reeled in; we could see their happy grins and one of them, through a cloud of smoke, gave a thumbs-up sign in our direction.

Although I didn't particularly like the style and attitude of those four anglers, I felt in a way happy for them because imagine what the long journey back to France would have been like without a fish: four disappointed, ill-tempered anglers in a car full of smoke. The thought alone made me shiver and before I could indulge in further idle altruistic empathy (which after all is easy when you have your brace of trout), we realised that there was something wrong. The angler was still holding on to the bent rod but you could tell from the hanging shoulders of his friends that something was amiss. Half a minute or so later we saw the reason for it: the angler and his friend landed a dead kid goat. The whirlpools and the undercurrents had pulled the kid goat under water at the neck of the pool. The angler then hooked it and for a short while was given the perfect illusion of a big fish on the hook. What an end to a fishing week! I felt really sorry for them now. Worst of all, they didn't see the funny side of it but at dinner Peter saw only that side and burst out in inordinately loud laughter when I related the events to him, and somehow I felt that the marmorata quartet knew what he had found so amusing. They were sitting at their table sulking in the filthiest of tempers, a cloud of smoke hanging over them...

But should I feel sorry for them as I did? After all, I didn't choose their attitude and tactics for them. They had come with a ready-made plan and didn't bother with local knowledge and didn't ask any of the other anglers in the hotel for advice. They weren't able to create a different state from which they could operate. You see, you have actively got to do something to get into the right state, and that something you've got to do is think. What exactly do I mean by this? What I am saying is:

1) The quartet had obviously left prudence at home. They rushed in with their *idée fixe* about how to proceed without reflecting a single moment about what they were confronted with. Prudence would have demanded a reappraisal of the conditions which might have led them to adopt a different approach and maybe even the prize they were after.

2) Their excessive self-imposed pressure blinded them to the piscatorial facts that were staring them in the face. They were thus incapable of adapting to the conditions.

3) Their impatience prevented them from taking a relaxed attitude, and this in turn prevented them from finding the least bit of enjoyment.

4) They lacked the courage to look at their situation in a radically different way. They were unable to critically assess themselves and their fishing tactics.

5) They failed to muster and apply their angling knowledge

Given all this, I really shouldn't feel sorry for them. Or had I neglected a duty by not drawing their attention to some obvious facts? I prefer to think that on their long way back they began to understand what went wrong and thus have become better and happier anglers. Perhaps they look back at the experience in Slovenia with a knowing and self-forgiving smile.

Short and to the point: The marmorata quartet completely failed to achieve the right interplay and balance of the angler's essential virtues: prudence, patience, moderation, and involvement. There is a little qualification as regards involvement, which is not a virtue in the same sense as the other three are. Involvement is more of an obligation on the contemporary angler – the current situation requires him to get involved in one way or another protecting and advancing angling. This wasn't the case in Walton's day, when angling wasn't threatened as it is today.

There were other problems in Walton's lifetime. The main one was the Civil War. Some modern readers might be tempted to feel that Walton was an escapist of a sort, turning his back on the world. I think this would be doing him a great injustice. Tranquillity as opposed to the hectic world is a theme running right through the story of mankind. I suspect that there must have been moments when a caveman yearned for a Xanadu on account of the rat race or a Xanthippe. The point is that what we perceive as a slow pace of life in, say, the 17th century seemed in those days to be breathtakingly fast, and the turmoil of the Thirty Years War in Europe and the Civil War in England were today's equivalent of terrorism, global warming, AIDS, hunger, drugs, violence and so on. Probably every period of history looked to its contemporaries as mad and threatening as the present age does to us today. The tranquillity yearned for is, however, essentially the same and that tranquillity then and now could be found in the beauty of angling. It isn't escapism to seek recreation but a necessity for "a state of complete physical, mental and social well-being" (from the WHO definition of health – it just goes to show you how much ahead of his time Walton was). Walton clearly talks of angling as not being a hermit-like withdrawal from the world:

Indeed, my good scholar, we may say of angling, as Dr. Boteler said of strawberries, 'Doubtless God could have made a better berry, but doubtless God never did'; and so, if I might be judge, God never did make a more calm, quiet, innocent recreation than angling.

"Recreation" is the key word because it implies that there is something to recreate from. Then and now that something can only be the mad state of the world, stress at work, troubles at home, depression, sorrows, burnout etc. The more enlightened don't wait until the world has worn them down – they go in for prevention; they break their daily routine by going fishing. Recreation, escapism, amusement: whatever the topics, the central theme is, however, the "more" of angling about which Bryn Hammond in his seminal *Halcyon Days* explains:

> *By 1676 and the publication of Walton's 5th edition, coupled with Cotton's first edition as Part 2 of The Complete Angler, going fishing became more of an event once again, and the sentiment Piscator non solum piscatur (there is more to fishing than catching fish) became not only acceptable, but the prime reason for fishing. In this respect Walton's influence was not only singular, but persists to this day and has permeated much of the vast literature on angling since that time.*

Regardless of the influence on angling literature or attitudes to angling, "there is more to fishing than catching fish" is, as I have suggested earlier on, a fact applying to all anglers at all times. "There is more to fishing than catching fish" is to angling what gravity is to physics. In his stimulating *Haunted by Waters* Mark Browning quotes the same passage from Hammond and continues:

> *Walton not only allows the reader to understand that there is more to fishing than catching fish, but also uses his text as a sort of parable of his particular version of Christianity. Interestingly, as the early Christians used the sign of the ιχθυζ to camouflage their activities, so does Walton some fifteen centuries later use fish to camouflage his Anglican spirituality.*

Like many other commentators, Browning can't resist the temptation to historicise over Walton, and he sets a breathtaking pace in those few lines. ιχθυζ stands for ICHTYS the initials of Iesous Christos, Theou Yios Soter meaning Jesus Christ, Son of God, Saviour. ICHTYS is the Greek word for fish and the fish became a Christian symbol or a symbol for Christians. The precise use of the symbol is subject to interpretation and ranges from the early Christians having a knack for acrostics to the symbol being a conspiratorial device, but it could never camouflage their activities. I fail to understand the meaning of "used the sign of ιχθυζ to camouflage their activities" and I also don't see the compelling link to *The Compleat Angler*. Browning surely can't mean that Walton went fishing so he could write *The Compleat Angler* as a parable. Walton was an angler, there is no doubt about that. Besides, what exactly is meant by "Anglican spirituality"? There certainly is nothing specifically Anglican about "wisdom", "learning", "knowledge" and "experience", to name but some of the main themes in *The Compleat Angler*. There's something fishy about this passage: too much, too quick. Browning then continues to contrast Walton's attitude with that of a later period:

A review of fishing literature published in the golden age of British angling, the Victorian and Edwardian periods, illustrates that while anglers in Walton's period might have truly subscribed to the Piscator non solum piscatur credo, those who came after either completely abandoned that ideal or relegated it so far behind the primary conflict between angler and fish that it disappears altogether from the literature.

"There is more to fishing than catching fish". That ideal might have disappeared from literature but hasn't gone away. The point I wish to make, however, is not to criticise Browning's book or that particular passage, but a general one. *The Compleat Angler* is in my view more philosophical than its form suggests and the tools of literary criticism might not entirely do justice to it as a piece of philosophy.

The perspicacious and perhaps more philosophically inclined Hammond has clearly understood that Walton and *The Compleat Angler* are more of an embodiment of angling than a particular episode in the history of literature, in general, and angling literature, in particular. The following is Hammond at his best:

After Walton's day one is led to believe that successive generations of anglers looked back with nostalgic longing, somehow seeing those idyllic and bucolic fishing days as being something that contemporary living could no longer provide. Right up to and including the time of the Industrial Revolution anglers looked wistfully backward to halcyon days long since gone – and to better fishing. It is my own suspicion that thus it ever was, and is likely to be: rear vision has a romance about it hard to resist; a lotus land where it was always yesterday. Maybe, after all, it hinges upon a dim race-memory of the Garden of Eden.

Brilliant. Note that the concluding statement applies to all times before and after Walton. I especially like the remark about the "rear vision". There is something colossally mystifying about "the good old days". Hardly anyone, it seems, is not charmed by the good old days. Even Neanderthal men probably looked sighingly back. This is absolutely amazing because on closer inspection the so-called good old days invariably turn out to be fairly bad old days. The typical example is that of people who suffered hardship, poverty and injustice in their youth but from the age of about fifty onwards, that hell of a time suddenly takes on a transformation.

Fishing days are, of course, the exception because as a popular rule has it there is no such thing as a bad fishing day. But is this true? What about the Soca days of the restless marmorata quartet who had no time or mind for pauses? Will their fishing at some future point seem like "good old days?"

The marmorata quartet are exemplary in many ways and also typical for a blind belief in action which more than anything upsets calm and quiet and certainly doesn't catch fish. That belief in activity might be a reflex fostered by an upbringing and education which simply leave no time for pauses. In the last twenty years or so many children were brought up on the assumption that they have to be entertained, i.e. children can't look after themselves or discover things on their own. There must always be something going on and consequently the diary of a four-year-old resembles that of a senior executive rushing from one meeting to another. "You can't be successful if you don't dash about like mad" is the attitude bred by hyper-parenting. The absence of reflection in the sense of evaluation – let alone contemplation – led the marmorata quartet to a pointless mechanical performance of acts of fishing. Without reflection or contemplation, fishing makes no sense and although Walton certainly hadn't activity fetishism in mind, his discussion of action and contemplation bears on it directly:

… I shall tell you that in ancient times a debate hath arisen and it remains yet unresolved: whether the happiness of man in this world doth consist more in contemplation or action?

Walton then briefly considers the merits of each and concludes:

Concerning which two opinions, I shall forbear to add a third, by declaring my own: and rest contented in telling you, my very worthy friend, that both these meet together, and do most properly belong to the most honest, ingenious, quiet and harmless art of angling.

Here is a piece of wisdom and truth – trying to get the balance right is indeed the key to the good angling life and the good life itself. If you want to catch fish, you have to get the balance right. Nobody said that this is easy; in fact it can be quite hard. You have to work for your fish, you have to work for your values. Now tell me which other pastime literally forces this truth on you? You're right; there is none. In this respect angling is absolutely unique.

What about the "good life" I have just mentioned – what exactly is the meaning of it? The good angling life is that which makes the angler happy. The good angling life, as "life" implies, doesn't however refer to one or a specific series of angling excursions, but to your whole life as an angler. During that life you aim for good / beautiful angling, that is, catching fish with sporting methods. In order to get what you're aiming at you employ knowledge, experience and reasoning. Reason guides you to good angling. Likewise, reason guides you to the good life (of which the good angling life forms a part). The good life is that which makes you happy, and reason leads us to the knowledge that the good of the good life is to live a virtuous life. That is the background and deeper meaning of the following passage from *The Compleat Angler*:

O sir, doubt not that angling is an art. Is it not an art to deceive a trout with an artificial fly? A trout! That is more sharp-sighted than any hawk you have named, and more watchful and timorous than your high mettled merlin is bold; and yet I doubt not to catch a brace or two to-morrow for a friend's breakfast: doubt not, therefore sir, but that angling is an art, and an art worth your learning. The question is rather, whether you be capable of learning it? For angling is somewhat like poetry, men are to be born so: I mean with inclinations to it, though both may be heightened by discourse and practice: but he that hopes to be a good angler, must not only bring an inquiring, searching, observing wit, but he must bring a large measure of hope and patience, and a love and propensity to the art itself; but having once got and practised it, then doubt not but angling will prove to be so pleasant, that it will prove to be like virtue, a reward to itself.

Izaac Walton

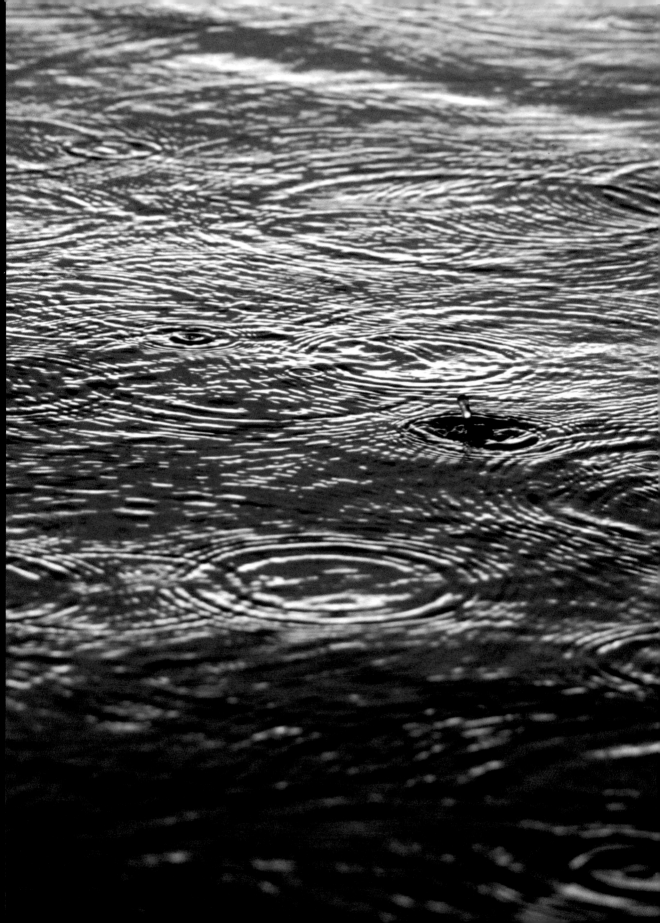

SPLASH, FLASH, BANG!

In the instant-gratification culture many people currently live in, the message of "learning", "hope" and "patience" sounds like something from another planet. By instant-gratification culture I mean an attitude which transcends Oscar Wilde's dictum "We know the price of everything but the value of nothing". In an instant-gratification culture there is not even a price let alone the notion of value for anything – or the other way round: everything is worthless. The best example of this "culture" is seen in parents who go to absurd lengths to provide instant gratification, success or make-believe success or achievement for their children, which is tantamount to opening the backdoor to nihilism. Nihilism, as I have mentioned earlier, basically means the rejection, denial and active destruction of values. Life is meaningless and there is no place for beauty or fishing in a nihilistic view of the world. The German philosopher Friedrich Nietzsche, was the most famous exponent of nihilism. His analysis that Western culture will be corroded by nihilism seems to be sadly accurate if you look around. Traditional values, especially in morals, seem at present to melt away more rapidly than butter in the sun.

Instant-gratification aborts any culture of "desirability" and poisons a child's future by robbing him of deliberation, happy anticipation and the pleasure and satisfaction of having genuinely achieved something. Instant gratification is an instance of nihilism. There is no consideration, evaluation, appreciation, deliberation, reasoning or thinking about the object (or state) of desire (is it desirable in the first place?). Everything becomes meaningless. Instant gratification is a sort of vegetative state and entails a throwaway mentality. I know this sounds a bit harsh and way over the top but it's not entirely unfounded. Nothing but nothing is of value any more – you can dump everything and everything is dumped, nobody cares, nobody wants to know. Having pointed to the nihilistic quagmire, let's look the other way now, where I can see rays of hope.

Isn't it the case that many people examine their attitudes, especially regarding the environment? In fact, the pendulum is swinging quite to the opposite extreme, which, however, is better than no movement at all. Fighting pollution unites in purpose people who are worlds apart and it does so on an intellectual and popular level. Oil spillage sights are an aesthetic insult to everybody, they upset and shock and show that people do believe and perceive values of a kind. That's surely a start and a promising one at that.

Fishing doesn't escape the instant-gratification mania but it can play the odd trick on the best of plans: Luke is the apple of his mother's eye. He was ten when he discovered fishing and that is what he wanted to do. Where he lived, he had to pass an exam in order to obtain a fishing permit. So Luke learned the basics of biology, water, fish, minimal sizes, bag limits and ... and duly passed his exam. He was delighted and rightfully so. Being ten, he had to have somebody to take him places and that somebody was his mum. After the second unsuccessful excursion, Luke's uncle happened to ring for a family reunion they had planned for the following week and found his sister all fluttered about Luke failing to catch a fish. His mum probably felt just how eagerly Luke wanted to catch a fish, which made her all impatient and nervous – the poor boy this, the poor boy that and in her mind's eye she probably conjured up a guilt scenario, whereby she would be to blame if the boy didn't catch a fish immediately. He would get an inferiority complex for the rest of his life. Luke's uncle, who was a client of mine and not an angler, tried to bring her down to earth by pointing out that this was what fishing was probably all about. She wouldn't listen to reason: a fish it had to be on the spot. Later that day mum happened to read a newspaper article about a fishery in a small mountain lake not too far away. Rainbow trout were helicoptered in and the highly critical article described how ridiculously easy it was to catch fish and asked what the sense of it was.

In next to no time the plans for the family reunion were altered to accommodate Luke's fishing. On the appointed day Luke, his dad and two uncles (with borrowed tackle) went fishing on that lake where the fish supposedly hurled themselves at the hook. All in all, there were about a dozen anglers there that day. Yet for some strange reason – nobody, but nobody – caught a fish all day and only practically with

148

the very last cast of the day (everybody else had already packed in) did Luke get his first and well-deserved fish. He was understandably over the moon with pride. His mum, equally happy, didn't give it a rest and immediately began to worry and fuss: there were ten people for that family reunion and there was no way that trout would feed ten people. She had assumed that the men would bring back enough trout for all. Thinking that little Luke might feel disappointed and to protect him from humiliation, she rushed to the fishmonger but apparently recovered her senses on her way there. She did an about-turn and cooked a dinner for ten people with the one trout as the main course. What a brilliant, glorious and wise idea! Each of the guests was presented with beautifully decorated morsel of Luke's catch (with lots of rice), and the verdict was unanimous: this was the best trout ever and toast upon toast was proposed to the lucky angler.

In this case fate averted instant gratification – only just. What luck for the boy. Just imagine if they had gone there and everybody had caught fish in masses as the newspaper article had suggested. What a tragic letdown this would have been. Maybe not at that particular moment but later on when, on reflection, Luke would have had to admit to himself that his fish wasn't really his first fish and that there had been no achievement. This more than anything else would have caused an inferiority complex or some other psychological anomaly. The fortuitous way Luke came by his first fish is undoubtedly an instance of the beauty of angling.

There is another angle on Luke's story which highlights a key feature of angling: it can't be done by proxy and you can't cheat yourself into thinking that you've been successful. In order to achieve, the effort has to be yours. Izaak Walton covers this aspect of angling with a little anecdote. The situation is that one of his pupils whom he is teaching to fish, "Venator", doesn't catch fish - while his teacher, Walton, does. Venator remarks that the tackle could account for the difference between success and failure. On this, Walton hands his rod to the pupil and continues fishing with Venator's rod. Walton keeps on catching trout while the pupil still tries in vain. Walton then relates the following to Venator:

A scholar (a preacher I should say) that was to preach to procure the approbation of a parish, that he might be their lecturer, had got from his fellow pupil the copy of a sermon that was first preached with great commendation by him that composed it: and though the borrower of it preached it, word for word, as it was at first, yet it was utterly disliked as it was preached by the second to his congregation: which the sermon-borrower complained of to the lender of it; and thus was answered:" I lent you, indeed, my fiddle, but not my fiddlestick; for you are to know that every one cannot make music with my words, which are fitted to my own mouth." And so, my scholar you are to know, that as the ill pronunciation or ill accenting of words in a sermon spoils it, so the ill carriage of your line, or not even fishing even a foot to the right place, makes you lose your labour: and you are to know, that though you have my fiddle, that is, my very rod and tacklings with which you see I catch fish, yet you have not my fiddlestick, that is, you yet have not skill to know how to carry your hand and line, or how to guide it to a right place: and this must be taught you (for you are to remember, I told you angling is an art) either by practice or long observation, or both.

Angling is real and is not virtual. It can't be modified at will. You can't cheat your way into a fish. And there is always the possibility of your honest effort not being rewarded. **Hope, patience, virtue, practice – all these notions seem to be terribly outdated.** And yet Izaak Walton's *The Compleat Angler* is one of the most frequently reprinted books in English literature. The reason for this is that truth, beauty and good are never outdated and are recognised or felt at all times. Walton's great achievement is to make wisdom accessible, to offer help in understanding what the good angler and the good life is. That is why I am convinced that Walton will be alive and kicking for centuries to come.

The virtuous angler will over time catch more fish than the angler who disregards or doesn't try to acquire the principal virtues of angling. Before looking at the main aspects of these, I emphasise that the neat listing of prudence, patience and moderation is misleading in the sense that none of these virtues is by itself a virtue. Only the interplay and balance of all these virtues gives them merit, just as the balance and interplay between bait, hook, line and fisherman must be right to catch a fish. When I was a student in Geneva, I

fished the Rhône there in the town itself where the river is corseted between streets and promenades using the cadre as the locals did. **The cadre is a wooden frame around which the line is wound.** As a beginner you lean over the railings and let down the baited hook (worm, grub, nymph or jig) and once in position, you begin to work the bait with your index finger... You feel the take, strike and the perch is yours. But not immediately: first you have to haul it up and get it over the railing, hoping that it's well hooked and doesn't fall off. The handline "pros" are great casters and the retrieval of line has to be seen to be believed: you don't wind in line more precisely with your fixed spool reel than those fishermen with their cadre. With superior skills on their side these fishermen regularly catch lovely trout.

Simple as it may seem, you have to get the balance and interplay right. If somebody tells you about the right line strength and the ideal hook size, that saves you a lot of time and frustration. **A lot of shared experience is in that simple balance of hook and line,** about which you can learn if you're willing. In the same way you can learn about angling virtues. The knowledge and the experience are there to be tapped but as in handline fishing, the acquisition and application of knowledge are your part of the deal. In this you might succeed at various times to various degrees, but by trying to get the balance and interplay right you will catch more fish and be a good angler.

The angling virtues must be seen as interdependent, interwoven and overlapping; what you are looking for is a harmonious balance between them, appropriate to the situation. This means that the balance of virtues is not static. Situation X might require more prudence than situation Y and an excess in the sense of "too much of a good thing" is just as detrimental to the right balance as the complete absence of any of the virtues. Excessive prudence will never help you catch a fish because, all things considered, it might be too risky to go fishing in the first place (you might get wet and catch a cold). Likewise, a complete lack of patience will never get a fish into the frying pan. Indvidual virtues can be characterised like individual players of a team:

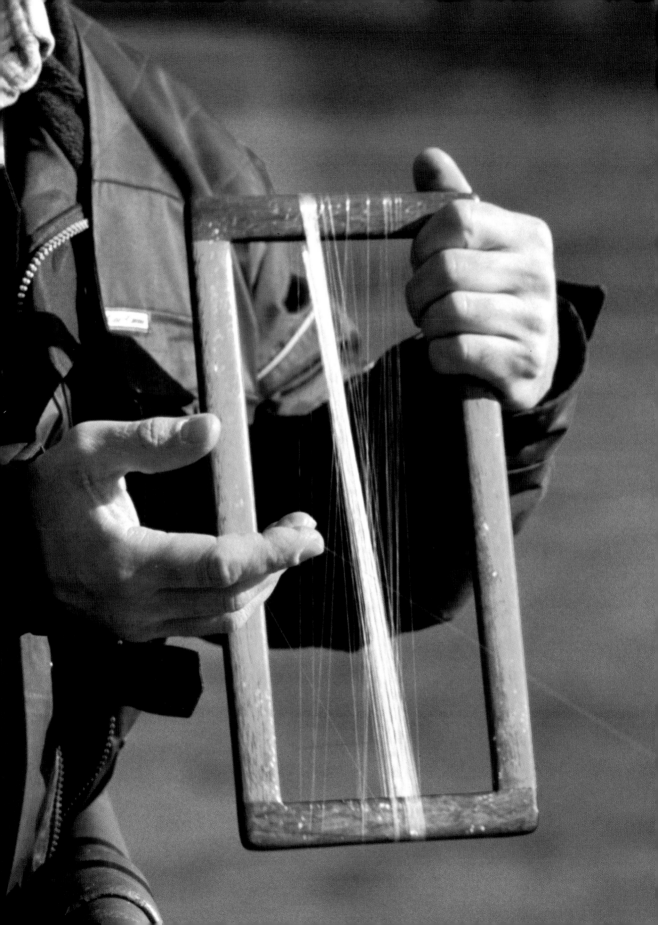

Prudence

Prudence begins with safety. Safety on boat and bank surely is the foremost concern. An angler who doesn't care about his safety or that of his fellow anglers can never be a good angler. Negligence in safety questions isn't part of good angling. Common sense is the best safety guide. However, it needs to be underpinned by knowledge: if you are unaware of the dangers, how are you to avoid them? So you have to learn about dangers, preferably not the hard way but by somebody telling you, which in turn means somebody is sharing his experience with you. Although fishing might be a one-man show there is no other sport which involves and presupposes so much common sense, commonly shared knowledge and communication.

Common sense should also guide all practical matters, of which too many go into angling to list here. All of them, however, involve critical and analytical thinking. Preparing a fishing holiday is infinitely more complex than, say, preparing a tennis holiday. In fact, just going fishing for a couple of hours is not without its pitfalls and requires a degree of organisation you wouldn't suspect. When the fishing urge gets the better of you, you tend to rush and overlook things: car doors left unlocked, car keys left in the boot, lights left on, forgotten waders, forgotten this that and the other. Most dedicated anglers try to keep the essential equipment in the boot. A look in the car boots of anglers shows the spectrum: There's the highly organised type like my friend Giovanni. His boot is like his glove compartment: everything has its proper place. I believe in an organised approach, but looking into my car boot reveals poorly disguised disorder. At the far end, so to speak, utter chaos reigns. The right and efficient way to do things is somewhere between, but getting there isn't as easy as it sounds. The problem of getting yourself organised was already known in Walton's day; he proposes verse in order to think of everything (*The Compleat Angler*):

> *My rod and my line, my float and my lead,*
> *My hook and my plummet, my whetstone and knife,*
> *My basket, my baits both living and dead*
> *My net, and my meat, for that is the chief:*
> *Then I must have thread, and hairs green and small,*
> *With mine angling-purse – and so you have all.*

There was a time when I was a regular rod junkie. My rod rack testifies to my former addiction and is a constant reminder of my weakness. Most of my rods are Sages with a lifelong warranty. If a rod breaks it is replaced, which means, my manifest inability to prudently steer around the rod rack at the tackle shop will be with me right through to my final reel-in. When I stood in the tackle shop in front of the of the rod rack my common sense seemed to evaporate. There I was looking at them, knowing I really didn't need another one. Yet at the same time I would think about that 10-footer which would be ideal for... and before you could say "hooked", I heard myself asking whether I could try it. And then more often than not I said, "to hell with it – other people have expensive girl friends" and would end up buying yet another rod. I am a bad advertisement for prudence or moderation in this respect, but I am happy to tell you that matters have improved dramatically since I started fly-tying a couple of years ago. I now go past the rods unaffected and head straight for the fly-tying section which holds other, equally fatal attractions.

Not following common sense advice can indeed be fatal. About thirty years ago I had a narrow escape in the valley of the Dordogne in the Périgord area of France. The Dordogne is a river of outstanding beauty in a region full of culinary and historic interest. Culinarily speaking, the Périgord is held by many as one of the world's richest regions. Not so much measured by the density of highly praised and expensive restaurants, but by the high average standard owing to the region's excellent products. I was there with my mother in a modest auberge in a small village. Humble the hostel might have been, but I assure you gastronomically it was fit for a king. Madame who was the chef, was a magician, a genius.

Fishingwise, pike was then foremost in my mind. I had done some research at home (immensely time-consuming in the pre-Internet days), and the landlord had assured me that indeed there were pike. Chatting with him I learnt that the thunderstorms there built up quite fast and that they were no joke at all. A couple of days later – I hadn't yet made contact with *Esox lucius* – I was at the river and the sultry late afternoon signalled a storm brewing. **I received the signal loud and clear and didn't do anything about it,** i.e. I didn't move. I was ignoring the telltale signs of the approaching thunderstorm. The reason for this was plain stupidity supported by a

completely irrational conviction that just before the thunderstorm fish
– in the present case pike – take best. As the landlord had promised,
the thunderstorm hit me in no time. Instead of running there and
then, I decided in superior foolishness to cast my spoon for the last
time. To this very day I can see the Toby fly out and splash into the
water. It could have been my very last cast forever. Splash, flash, bang
– lightning hit the river ten yards in front of me. The shock or the
air pressure or both lambasted me, and so I must have staggered
backwards and fallen into the bushes on the bank. I woke up wet but
all limbs accounted for and not a single bump or scratch.

The thunderstorm had passed and it was bright again. As I slowly
recovered my senses I realised I was still gripping my fishing rod. I
got back on my feet and started to reel in and suddenly felt a solid
resistance: the pike that was on must have taken while I was staggering
backwards. The jerking, uncontrolled random movement probably
made the Toby irresistible. I safely landed a small pike of about five
pounds, which made a superb dinner for my mother and me and some

other guests at the hostel. This whole incident sounds cooler than it was, as apparently I was white as a sheet and shaking when I returned to the hostel. It was put down to the excitement of the catch. I didn't say anything about the close shave I had just experienced, but believe me the shock had a lasting impact. To this very day I get frightened by thunder and lightning and have to grit my teeth not to pack in and run immediately after the first rumbling noises.

Some really awkward situations can arise when prudence is thrown to the winds. The other day I was fishing with my friend Roland (the Swiss Roland, not the Belgium Roland) on the Zwingsee near Inzell in upper Bavaria. The Zwingsee is a tiny gem of a lake fed by alpine springs. The water is crystal clear but before I get to the beautiful trout that are in it, I have to sketch the setting so that you can fully appreciate the series of events that took place on that particular day. The lake is roughly an isosceles triangle some 300 yards from the base to the apex. The base itself is about 150 yards wide. The upper end of the lake features a lovely mix of reeds and undergrowth and to the left and the right of it are two small, steep, rocky and pine-studded hills giving the scene a theatrical touch. The hills convey an impression of massiveness because the lake is so small. This pure opera set of natural splendour contrasts starkly with the landscape in the opposite direction. There, instead of Wagnerian alpine drama, is a stadium for speed-skating and in front of it a car park. If you stood on the base of the triangle and looked mountainwards again, there was on the left of the base a restaurant (which is now closed) with tables right at the waterfront. The tables were arranged in two rows (maybe twenty in all). It was a great place to eat out and paradise for the trout, because people had fun feeding them all sorts of morsels straight from their plate. Moreover, in the holiday season there would be coaches stopping to marvel at this little treasure of a lake, and people immediately spotted the trout and fed them with whatever there was at hand from the car park.

Wise to this, the trout continuously patrolled the margins at the base of the lake expecting and getting food. There couldn't be many better-fed trout in the world than those at the lovely Zwingsee – they were the Kobe beef of trout. The car park is separated from the lake by a fence, and between the fence and the water runs the bank from where anglers can cast their line These pampered gourmet-glutton trout are laughing at your flies. Special tactics are required here.

Roland and I were trying our luck there with our backs to the car park. It was the peak holiday season and lots of walkers and coaches were stopping by. We patiently answered a thousand times the same questions and realised that under these circumstances fishing is a spectator sport. We certainly got enough roll-casting practice because there was no way you could back cast for fear of hooking an onlooker. Anyway, we had fished unsuccessfully for a couple of hours and it was getting towards midday. It was particularly frustrating because you see the prize you're after all the time, right there, in front of you. They were big, strong trout of great culinary value. **When the fishing is slow, the mind sometimes wanders** miles away from where you are and what you're doing (is this good angling?). With "I've got one", Roland shook me out of my daydream. As I looked over, I saw him into a big fish. I had the net with me and without thinking I put my rod down and ran over to Roland. What a stupid thing to do! First of all Roland was only about ten yards away from me so there was no need to rush. It was a strong fish which wouldn't be ready for a while. There would have been plenty of time for me to reel in or to secure the rod properly. In the event, I did nothing of the sort. I had hardly taken two steps when Roland shouted, "Watch out!", nodding in the direction of the abandoned rod. I turned round only to see it disappear into the water. Petrified, I stood there not believing my eyes: this happens in cartoons, not in real life, I thought. It was all real enough though. "The net..." Roland reminded me. I managed to apply myself to the task of landing the fish with Roland and then assessed the situation. It wasn't difficult: the trout had dragged my rod right in front of those twenty tables, not one of which was vacant! There some twenty yards from the shore the tip stuck out like a sore thumb. The trout had shaken the barbless hook off and planted the rod firmly at that particular spot.

There was nothing for it but to swim there and get it. The water was icy (it's cold enough for char) and as luck would have it, the very moment I started to undress two coaches arrived at the car park, spilling out literally hundreds of people. It wasn't long before some of the day-trippers realised that something extraordinary was afoot and alerted their fellow travellers. To hell with it – in I went

160

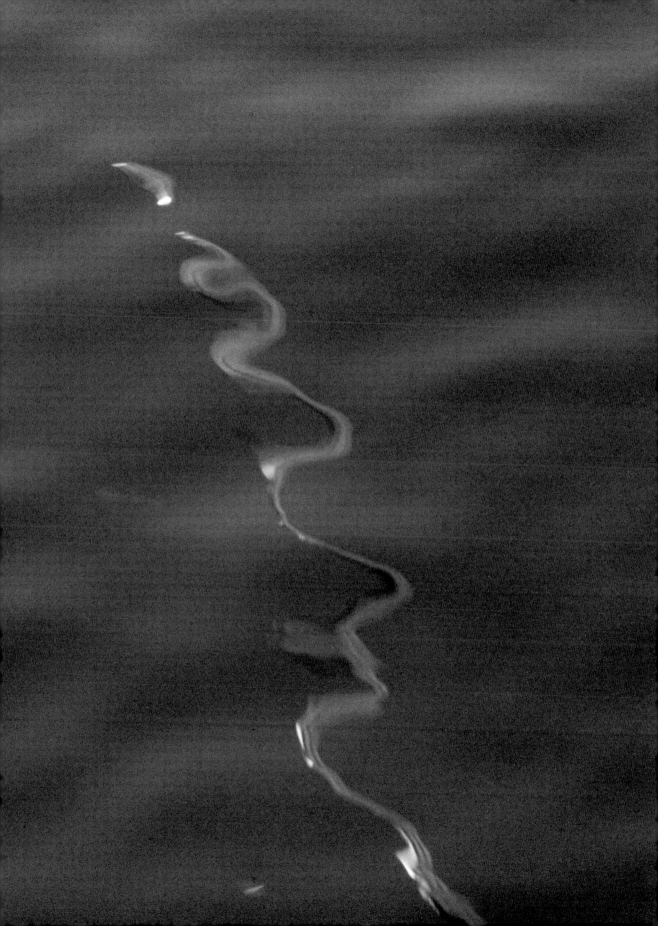

and swam the forty yards or so to the rod before hundreds of pairs of eyes. My efforts were greeted by the cheers and gesticulations of the restaurant guests. As I approached the rod, somebody had the glorious idea of throwing bread crumbs in my direction. In the ensuing feeding frenzy, a trout actually jumped over my head to be in on the food melee at the other side of me. I swam the last twenty yards in a crowd of excited trout and finally grabbed my rod and started to reel in. I hardly had made to turns when the fly was violently taken by a huge trout.

What a predicament! The spectators cheered and as water carries sound so well, I could even hear some of the comments. The most humiliating was a child asking, "Mummy what's that man doing there?" "Well…er…er…fishing, of course," was her answer. There was, however, no time for rejoinders. I had a fish, and silly situation or not, I intended to keep it. Swimming the backstroke just with my legs I played that fish until I managed to hand over the rod to Roland. Then I nipped out of the water, took the rod back and together with Roland landed a beautiful four-pound rainbow. Applause accompanied the final stages. I have hardly ever felt so embarrassed and mortified, but I grinned and bore it. Funny and comic as it all might have been, though, there is such a thing as professional pride. I am sure you know what I mean: it just shouldn't happen that way. Roland's comment summed it up neatly: "If you carry on like that, you'll make the headlines of the national papers." The Zwingsee isn't, of course, always that busy – this was an exceptional day. The restaurant may not exist anymore but the Zwingsee can still be fished and it is still as hard as ever to persuade those beautiful trout.

Patience

"I wouldn't have the patience for it," non-anglers often say, and by that they usually mean that they couldn't sit for hours on a riverbank trying to hypnotise a float. Patience in this usage means waiting. But concentrating on a float is more than waiting for a bus. You know the bus will (eventually) come and take you from point A to point B. There are few imponderables when waiting for a bus, whereas watching a float is surrounded by uncertainties and expectations.

162

When you've got a float to watch, there always
seems to be a prospect of something happening
immediately."

The Float, Keith Harwood

"Something happening immediately" – the non-angler will never perceive a float in that way. Whereas the angler is able to sustain the expectation for hours. The inexperienced angler does so by banking on a vague hope of a fish taking, whereas the experienced angler's expectation is built on knowledge. His angling knowledge reveals to him the potential of an angling situation and that fuels his imagination, i.e. builds up his expectation. Patiently queuing for a bus is a passive routine, the boredom of which one tries to break by reading a newspaper or making completely pointless phone calls. Patiently watching a float is exciting action with a purpose, as millions of anglers will confirm.

In the meadows of my youth there was a most peculiar man, whom I nicknamed "Attila the Hun" because he was a man from Hungary. He was a firm believer in "big bait, big fish". At the time he was about fifty or sixty, which to a 14-year-old was as old as Methuselah. Besides the doctrine of "big bait, big fish" there were other iron laws to which he adhered. Over all the years I knew him, he fished the very same spot. That spot he chose not because it was the most promising, but because it was closest to the parking. He clearly didn't believe in undue exertion: his most important piece of equipment was a foldable chair, probably the biggest and most comfortable foldable chair on the market at that time. Attila sat there facing the river, proud as a king on his throne. The regalia displayed were a rod, a net, a box and an umbrella – not a big fishing umbrella, just a plain black umbrella. **There he sat, day in day out all season, from 4pm until nightfall.** Only the heaviest of thunderstorms would prevent him from taking up residence in his outdoor palace. He reigned uncontested over that particular spot. All the other fishermen respected his claim to it, probably not least because it wasn't deemed very promising.

Attila was a friendly man, good humoured and most eager to talk. The opening line of every conversation would be a variation of "The only method is big bait, big fish, you'll see." Then he would let himself be carried away by any old subject under the sun. He would go on and on and on, never taking his eyes off the float. He always used pike floats although he didn't fish for pike, and always fished close to the bank. I say he didn't fish for pike but he didn't fish for anything specific except a big fish. His bait was invariably a huge

lump of bread on what looked to me more like a meat hook than an angling hook, and with the line he used he could have pulled in a whale. Unwaveringly, he stuck to his guns year in year out, convinced, no, knowing – that one day he would catch a big fish and that this could happen at any moment, which is why he didn't take his eyes off the float. Talking to me as he did was highly irritating because he was an adult and I didn't dare to move on while he was addressing me. I stood there two or three times, not knowing what to do, keeping Attila company to nightfall. Evading that particular spot was also time-consuming, but less so. One day I decided not to bypass it because it would be getting dark before long. As I approached, I could see another fisherman standing there, listening to Attila's voice babbling on.

They hadn't seen me coming, and just before I reached them the fisherman bade a loud and clear "Tight lines!" and simply moved on. Attila stopped his monologue and replied with a hearty "Tight lines!". Aha. Seconds later, I arrived on the scene and Attila cast his conversational net over me. There I stood again. After about five minutes I plucked up all the courage I could and also bade a loud and clear "Tight lines!" before moving on. To my utter amazement and relief, it worked and I was on my way. From then on, Attila was no problem any more and I could always listen for as long as I was interested and then go about my business. Time passed and real life drew me away from those meadows.

Years later I learned from a friend that Attila had eventually caught a 20-pound carp and had had the fish stuffed at great expense. A carp that size was unheard of and even made it to the local newspaper. I can only assume it was caught on that same tackle he always used. Later that year I bumped into Attila on a train. We recognised each other immediately. He was around seventy then but mentally as fit as ever, and his first words after the exchange of greetings were: "I told you, didn't I: big bait, big fish" (taking it for granted that I knew!). To me it seemed more like "big wait, big fish". From what he told me, I could work out that he must have fished the better part of eight years for that carp. Did he catch other fish? I don't know. He kept on talking about that big one for the whole part of the journey we spent together.

What do you make of that? By ordinary angling standards Attila's approach was as unusual as it was unproductive. On the other hand, he got the big fish he wanted to catch and he got him "his way". Attila's carp could be classified as a freak catch but I for one don't regard that fish in such a light. In my view Attila knew that perseverance and patience would eventually succeed and that the good can take its time.

Moderation

In a fishing-holiday report from Canada published on the internet, I read that "... the graylings rose so freely, we tried our fly boxes for flies which they didn't take." Now that's an interesting statement telling a lot about the fishing and the anglers. It is clear that the fishing must have been out of this world, with grayling superabundant. So the anglers had either caught and kept or released many graylings, and **their conscience told them that it was enough** but they wanted to continue fishing and did the absurd by trying not to catch a fish. Under the circumstances, trying not to catch fish sounds like an ingenious way out of the dilemma of knowing that you should stop but wishing you could continue. On scrutiny, however, they should have stopped fishing. They knew they should stop. When you know something to be wrong, you should apply that knowledge and do whatever is required. This is often easier said than done – I didn't stop fishing the Dordogne even though I knew full well that a storm was brewing. Look at it from the moral angle and it was wrong, look at it from the safety angle and it was wrong. It was simply wrong on all counts and there is no excuse for it.

Another intriguing item I read on the web was from an angler who wants to devise barbless hooks which snap. The idea is that you feel the take but when the fish starts to run, a spring or something in the bend of the hook snaps and straightens it. By pulling, the fish releases itself. The hook can then be reset (I have no idea how this could work but if somebody puts his mind to it…). Now that's food for thought – if our anglers had had such hooks they could have continued fishing because the fish wouldn't even know they had been caught, but the anglers would know. No need for moderation then because you no longer catch fish. On the other hand such a hook defeats the whole idea of fishing because the object of the exercise is to catch fish and the process is an integral one. The object in fishing with hooks that automatically straighten themselves is not to catch a fish. You want to raise a fish; you want to induce a take, but you don't want to catch fish. This isn't fishing any more, is it?

Moderation in the tackle shop is a tricky subject.

As I have admitted, I myself have some real problems there. Is it really true that I definitely do not need another rod? Think: I also like books and as I have hundreds of them, why not also claim that I definitely don't need another book? "Ah," you might say "but books are different; each book is different". But doesn't the same apply to fishing rods? Just as I take a book out of the bookshelf to read it, I take a rod out of the rack to fish with it. And just as I have books on poetry and history, I have rods for pike and salmon and I can only fish with one at a time. Moreover, there are books in my bookshelves which I read years ago and may never read again. I have a rod which I have bought especially for fishing the flats – if I don't get round to fishing the flats any more, it will be waiting there like the book. The fact that one can read only one book at a time doesn't prevent one buying another book. In fact,

most people would think it outrageous to suggest that they shouldn't buy another book because they already have one. Why then should I restrain myself in the tackle shop? Each rod I buy, I buy with a purpose (however vague) and a curiosity (how does it fish?) in mind, which is very similar to buying a book. Provided I am not ruining my family or myself with books and rods, can there be excess in the first place? If there can't, there is no need for moderation, is there? I can't see a flaw in this argument, can you?

Some thirty years ago I followed my rod to Finland with what was called the Inter-rail ticket. With that ticket you could travel on all trains throughout Europe for a specified time. My plan was to fish for pike in the Finnish Lakeland area. With little luggage and high hopes I set out for the promised pike land and arrived at a little town called Pieksämäki. There I enquired about the fishing possibilities (again, these were pre-internet days) in the region and was stunned by the distances involved. Although I had considered the distances at home, on the spot it looked somehow unreal to walk for miles and miles and miles through the woods. The friendly man at the railway station, clearly understanding the problem, suggested that I should try and hitchhike to a "camping" some distance north. There, he said, I would find a couple of promising lakes near the road. I immediately got a lift from a lorry and the driver nodded when I showed him the piece of paper on which the man from the station had written the destination. The road stretched straight as a ruler through the endless woods and disappeared on the horizon.

I can't remember how long we drove, but somewhere in the middle of nowhere the lorry stopped. We had met practically no traffic because it was Sunday and, besides, this was not a main artery: it was a minor road. There was nothing there but wood (it must have been there that "not seeing the wood for the trees" was thought of) and a little track which the lorry driver said would lead to the "camping". I have to confess I felt a little anxious seeing the lorry drive away and get smaller and smaller before vanishing in the shimmering distance. There was a little wind on my back, just enough to move the branches of the trees and to produce a little creaking noise here and there. The track wasn't as straight as the main road. All I could see of it were the first two or three hundred yards and then, for no apparent reason, it bent sharply so that I was walking towards a wall of somber-looking pine trees. Beyond the first two or three rows of trees it was as dark as in a cow's stomach. Even though there was no sign posting of any kind I trusted the friendly man at the railway station and the lorry driver and walked deeper into the wood. After what seemed an eternity (probably a mile), the trees were less dense and there was the lake and the campsite. What a relief and what a beautiful sight that lake was! It looked so pristine, inviting and promising; its ripples cast lightwaves onto the trees. There were a couple of small caravans and a few tents and I was greeted with curiosity. The fishing rod, however, was self-explanatory and before long we sat there on heavy wooden benches and at an equally heavy wooden table discussing fishing in a mix of English, German and sign language. "We", included a cheerful group of young Finns spending their weekend camping. They invited me to eat and drink with them. Their tipple looked like milk and it was milk – mixed with vodka and sugar. A diabolical concoction. **I drank carelessly, thoughtlessly, stupidly** and was carried along by the jovial atmosphere. It was a mild, clear summer night and communication problems waned in inverse proportion to the drink consumed. As it was Sunday some people left, while others apparently planned to leave the following morning. Whatever, the effect of the drink was

disastrous. The moment I tried to stand up, I suddenly got all dizzy and my legs gave way. I can't remember how I managed to crawl into my sleeping bag, but in I got. The next morning was the most awful morning of my life. I was shaking hands with death and for more than one reason: the alcohol alone could have killed an elephant but as I managed to activate that little bit of brain that was still faintly working, I surmised that there was something even worse than the alcohol. The pain was not just that hangover-thumping headache. There was an intense burning sensation all around my body but especially painful, almost beyond endurance, around my face and head. I decided to splash water on my face and staggered to the lake. As I took off my shirt and looked at my arms, chest and belly I saw the reason for my agony: I was covered with insect bites. They were partly midges bites and partly wasp stings – I had slept on a wasps' nest and they are quite vindictive when you disturb their home.

There is nothing but shame for me in this story. The only, but only, bright spot is that I didn't completely panic when I became fully aware that I was all alone. Nobody there but the lake and smouldering embers. The explanation for this is straightforward: when the friendly man at the station said "camping", I thought he meant a regular campsite with infrastructure, which is why I had bought only a bottle of water before hitchhiking. This campsite was simply a popular meeting point with no infrastructure at all except for the benches and the table. Anyway, I resolved not to faint and to get back to the main road. Before that, however, I sat for some twenty minutes in that lake to cool down. The water had a soothing effect but, of course, I couldn't stay immersed all day. I got my bits and pieces together and made for the road. That walk was a pure nightmare: pain raced around my thumping head, which at various stages I believed was going to crack open and erupt like a volcano. My legs were leaden and my breathing heavy. Step by step I dragged myself towards that road and the most hellish moments were when the fear of dying tried to weaken my resolve to reach the road. I reached it and fainted.

I remember coming round for a short while in the passenger seat of a lorry, explaining in sign language to a worried driver what had happened only to fall back into a stupor. The kind man brought me to a doctor where I received emergency treatment. Then I was transferred to a room in the local hotel, where I slept apparently for more than 24 hours attended by the manageress who acted as a nurse. The doctor came to see me twice more, and after three days I had sufficiently recovered to be released into the world again. I asked for the bill (the doctor's and the hotel's) fearing that I didn't have enough money, but nobody would hear of it. The manageress, spoke German and explained that they regarded my treatment as a matter of course.

The first question you'll be asking is why did those people abandon me there. To this there can only be one explanation: they weren't aware of my state. They probably interpreted my heavy sleeping as natural under the circumstances and besides, I had said I wanted to stay there at the lake to fish. They thought nothing of it and left me to sleep there. They simply didn't know that there was something more than alcohol involved. Had it been alcohol alone, I would have had a very bad time next morning but nothing on the scale I actually experienced. The blame for the entire course of events is fairly and squarely on my shoulders – I brought this on myself. There was on my part no prudence, no moderation, no nothing which would have prevented that awful experience. The only marginally mitigating circumstance is that I wasn't aware of the potency of that mix. You see the reason for mixing the vodka with milk and sugar most likely was that the vodka was rough and not legal – Finnish poteen, so to speak. I had noticed that the vodka came in plain bottles and not in brand bottles, but I was not alert enough and did not draw the right conclusion. The consequence was that, instead of pursuing beautiful pike, I was escaping near-death.

Involvement

Ligula intestinalis is the reason why active involvement isn't exactly one of my fortes. But before turning to *Ligula intestinalis*, I would like to say what involvement ideally consists of. Involvement in the angling context means that the good angler takes an interest in the broad international issues, such as pollution, environment and animal welfare. On the other hand, what is happening is happening locally and is of prime importance. A good angler does participate in one way or another in the activities of an angling club. My active involvement is passive, so to speak, because I support the local club

financially. I must confess, I have great difficulty associating myself actively with a club, fishing or otherwise. The reason for this is what a psychologist would probably call the local- angling-club trauma. What happened? When I was about fourteen, I took an enthusiastic interest in all aspects of fish biology. I was simply curious and my parents supported this by buying me some expensive specialist books. One of them dealt exclusively with fish diseases and although it was way over my level, the drawings and pictures gave me a fair idea of what could happen to fish and why. As it happened, I caught various roach at that time which were clearly afflicted with *Ligula intestinalis.*

Ligula is a tapeworm that infests fish such as roach, dace and rudd. This tapeworm grows to incredible size in the fish. Instances are reported where the weight of the tapeworm has exceeded that of the fish! When the fish is weakened, it gets – ideally, from the tapeworm's point of view – eaten by a bird. The life cycle of *Ligula* starts in birds, where it lays its eggs and via the droppings then gets

174

into the water where it is eaten by copepods, which in turn are part of the fish diet.

Before my juvenile eye I saw an epidemic, thousands of dying and dead fish. But I also saw myself as the hero in this story, alerting people to the threatening calamity right on their doorstep. I was of course convinced that once the right people saw what was happening, they would act. I had no idea how but they would know how, wouldn't they? And who better than the men from the local angling club? After all, who could have a bigger interest in this disease than the fishermen? I approached this systematically and made a plan. The plan was to catch at various points tapeworm-stricken fish and record the place, time and size. Then I would dissect them and present them in two preserving jars in formaldehyde (I think it was). One sample would show an entire swollen-up fish, and the other a *Ligula* on its own – neither exactly a feast for the eyes. In this I eventually succeeded and then rang the president of the angling club, asking him whether I could come to a meeting to show my findings. He didn't have a clue what *Ligula* was but invited me to come along to the next meeting. *Ligula* being my preoccupation then, I found it strange that the president of an angling club didn't know about it and decided to take my book on fish disease along.

On the day I packed the preserving jars and the book in a bag and felt very pleased with myself, expecting interested anglers who would commend me for my vigilance and effort. I was all excited and looking forward to it. The meeting took place in a very low, shabby back room of a pub. As I opened the door, I hit a wall of smoke which was so thick you couldn't have cut it with a knife – you would have needed a chainsaw. Opening the door had created a little draught, so that as I stood in that doorway, wafts of smoke passed by me mixed with the unmistakable smell of schnaps. In the dimly lit room I could make out about a dozen or so faces, in all of which a cheap cigar or a cigarette was stuck. The men sat in groups of four at tables where slates and chalk were ready for playing cards. I heard a grunt, which signified, "Close the door". I perceived a dull hostility in the atmosphere and to this day I think that in comparison I would probably find a face-to-face with an inquisitor or a KGB-interrogation specialist in a dungeon a delightful encounter. Somewhere out of the nicotine fog a figure materialised, whom I assumed to be the president of the club. He didn't introduce himself; he just muttered a sound which I optimistically interpreted as a greeting and then motioned me to a table where there was a free chair. Intimidated as I was by the atmosphere of antipathy, I could feel my enthusiasm for presenting *Ligula* dwindling away quickly. The president opened the meeting, mentioning that a visitor was present who had something to show them. He then told me to put "it" on the table, which I did. There they were: the two preserving jars and the beautiful work I had done was finally on show. But nobody wanted to see it, really. A few craned necks and a corresponding few grunts – that was all.

No curiosity, no questions, no nothing. Everybody was obviously waiting to begin playing cards and hardly had the president finished the last point on the agenda than the cards were out. Taking this as a cue that the meeting was over, I packed up the *Ligula* and crossed the antechamber of purgatory over to where the president sat in order to say goodbye. Imagine now my shock when I recognised at the table none other than that stupid bailiff, that incarnation of blockheadedness and ignorance who had wrongly fined me only months ago. Here was the source of the hostility which I had felt all along. I hadn't spotted him before because of my excitement and the smoke and because he sat with his back to me. He sported a malicious grin and for a moment I feared he would address me. He didn't and I made for the door. Finally out in the fresh air, I felt a relief, the intensity of which I can sense even today when I recall the events. I inferred from the experience that all clubs must be like this one and resolved never ever to join one. My determination hasn't weakened since. The clubs that I am sort of associated with (the local angling club and the local yodelling club) I support financially which, technically speaking, probably makes me nevertheless a member of those clubs.

Now you might say that 35 years is a long time and that surely my personal angling-club trauma is of less importance than the cause of angling and that I should actively participate. Of course you're right and most likely the atmosphere in most angling clubs is different from what I experienced. It was just plain bad luck to fall in with such a rotten bunch. Nevertheless, once bitten twice shy. I still prefer to keep a distance and I reason that by generously supporting angling causes I do more good than by a half-hearted attendance at

club meetings. Also, I actively contribute by introducing youngsters of relatives and acquaintances to angling.

I have said that involvement isn't a virtue in the strict sense, but more an obligation on the contemporary angler, because angling and other fieldsports and countryside activities are threatened. The other day I had a lively after-dinner discussion with my angling friend Bill. He put it to me that surely there was absolutely no way that angling is going to be banned because the economic interest is too important and moreover, he maintained, it would be political suicide if a government proposed a ban on angling, precisely because of the negative economic impact and the 4 million active anglers (votes) in the UK. Bill then suggested that my warnings amounted to scaremongering and that the few beard-stroking crackpots who want to abolish angling will never get anywhere. Bill's view reflects at first sight good common sense, but I think it is short-sighted and parochial.

Earlier on I mentioned the ban sequence of hunting, shooting, fishing as being the political aim and tactics of the antis. The source of anti-hunting, anti-shooting and anti-angling is the same: animal rights. The openly declared aim of the animal-rights movement and its political support in the UK (and elsewhere) is first the abolition of hunting, then shooting and finally angling. Essentially, the arguments against hunting are the arguments against shooting and fishing. As long as anti-hunting isn't getting anywhere, angling will be safe. Unfortunately, Bill and other anglers fail to see this simple and obvious point, or perhaps they don't want to see it because they are indifferent to hunting or don't like people who hunt. I have met anglers who see in anti-hunting an opportunity for a revival of the class struggle. To put it politely this is very, very short- sighted because those anglers are helping to dig their own grave. I have to point it out again: if at present it weren't political suicide to abolish angling, it would be abolished overnight. **The political will to abolish all fieldsports is real.**

Not just in the UK, but all over Europe. In Germany animal rights have already made it to the constitution:

...paragraph 20a of the basic law now says that animals, like humans, have the right to be respected by the state and to have their dignity protected" (Guardian, Saturday June 22, 2002).

Constitutionally speaking this gives animals more rights than children have and also shows how the "crackpot" ideas of obscure philosophers suddenly materialise and change the real world. Let me remind you of the animal-rights philosopher who is the source of all this "dignity and respect" smoke screen, Tom Regan. When asked which he would save if a boat capsized in the ocean: a dog or a baby, he answered, "If it were a retarded baby and a bright dog, I'd save the dog". Just think!

The campaign to make the German law the European standard is well under way, and think again what "dignity protected" means. A fish is an animal and thus entitled to having its dignity protected. It doesn't need a lawyer to understand that a fish on a hook is a violation of the constitution. The point is to understand that the abolition of hunting, shooting and angling is an international issue

178

and while everything locally might look calm, a storm might be in the making elsewhere. Incidentally, beekeeping can't possibly be in line with the "dignity" of bees. Isn't exploiting bees for honey an insult to their dignity? A ban on angling doesn't look likely right now, but did it ever look more likely?

Science fiction? Hardly: in the Netherlands at the time of writing (September 2003) **a ban on angling for children under sixteen was discussed.** Just to be sure, we're talking not about a debate in an obscure animal-rightist journal but at the Parliamentary level.

The bottom line of this proposed ban is exemplary. The following text is taken from a Dutch website (http://www.animalfreedom.org/nietindehaak/english/faq.html#sportvissers_wreed):

The most experienced fisherman causes pain and stress to fish just by fishing. This is often multiplied when children fish, because of their inexpertness. In their innocence and ignorance, children disrupt nature; they do not recognise vulnerable plants and animals. Noisily, excitedly and roughly they move along the waterfront and make themselves a spot to fish from. A competition is a match in which the object is to catch as many or as big a fish as you can. The child is given the message that animals can be used for games, and that their interests are not important. Respect for nature also means respect for fish. Shouldn't adults give children the message that they should respect fish and so leave them alone?

A ban on angling for children under sixteen is tantamount to an overall ban on angling. If under-sixteen-year-olds must respect fish and leave them alone, what's the justification for allowing over-sixteen-year-olds to fish? Besides, fishermen are made between the ages of ten and fifteen: a ban would create a fatal lack of new blood. Rarity is the precursor to extinction. But lets have a look at some other points of this convoluted statement.

How can children disrupt nature? They're part of it and quite literally behave like nature's children. They're supposed to be curious and excited and are supposed to live their experiences in nature. Years back when we went for the first time to the Seychelles,

I watched boys not older than five or six fishing with handlines on the beach. There in the last wave, in hardly five inches of water were little fish, thousands of them, which the boys tried to catch. Having caught a fish they clumsily handled it and then released it or put it on the sandy beach to take home. When I saw this I immediately fell into the European concern trap. "What's the point of this?" I asked myself, conditioned by European angling conventions and forgetting how messy my first angling years were, until I reached a certain level of competence. I did as a boy exactly what those boys on the beach did and, as a consequence got stung, cut and hurt – but I learned something. **Killing a fish is not as easy as it sounds.** Take the boy who catches his first perch. Even though he's been warned that he can get stung by the perch's fins, he will get stung a dozen or more times until he knows how to handle the perch. He will accidentally let the perch drop and in trying to get hold of it again, the boy will invariably get stung. Then, on his knees, reaching for the flapping perch, he will knock over the can with the worms or, worse, break the rod by crawling over it.

He will eventually get hold of the fish: what now? Knock it on the head: yes, but what with? By the time the boy has come to grips with the perch and decided on a course of action, the fish is already dead. A smaller or greater number of perch later the boy knows how to handle and kill them but he couldn't possibly have got there without learning the hard way. This means accepting that along the way there will be clumsily handled fish. Baiting the hook, catching the fish and killing it (or releasing it for whatever reason) is clearly not a game like football, and yet there can be a competitive element in it. Like the boys on the beach in the Seychelles, I also competed with other boys and wanted to catch more fish than they did. Organising a fishing competition is nothing other than channelling the competitive element and the fishing urge in a controlled direction.

Youth violence is an issue all over Europe, and I must touch on it briefly because it concerns the angling question. The politically correct crowd sweeps violence away as non-existent, it pretends that violence is not part of human culture. Violence when it occurs in private and public is blamed on a variety of factors, the scope of which invariably includes racism, colonialism (the West is evil, the rest is good), capitalism, Christianity and, last but not least,

182

an antiquated understanding of nature – especially our treatment of animals. In the politically correct world, nature simply cannot be red in tooth and claw; it must be cruelty-free, cosy and full of New Age harmony. Man should of course not disturb that harmony, especially not with angling. Such an unrealistic attitude breeds a hypocritical atmosphere in which boys fighting and girls quarrelling are incidences of youth violence, prompting the interventions of psychologists, sociologists, social workers and other do-gooders. The same crowd screams blue murder at any disciplinary measures. The cultivation of an artificial non-violent climate involves toleration of any old thing, however wrong, and the wrongdoer usually gets out of it unscathed just as the perpetrator of a crime often turns out to be the victim. Short and to the point: the promotion of the politically correct cruelty-free society provokes violence because right and wrong are getting more and more veiled and they can no longer be distinguished. If you don't know what and where the limits are, you step over the line even without being conscious of it!

I bet young fishermen are a rarity in juvenile courts. Fishing involves knowledge and discipline. Even the most fidgety child understands that it has to stick with the rod in order to catch a fish. You've got to be there and concentrated on what you're doing. As a boy learning to fish, you immediately become aware that there are rules governing fishing and that those rules are binding. Not knowing that there are indeed rules and that they make sense and that breaking them will have consequences is, without a doubt, one of the prime causes of juvenile delinquency. If as a child you're led to believe there are no rules or values, except for those hazy ideas about a cruelty-free world, then as a young adult you'll be unable to recognise values. Fishing teaches you to recognise values, fishing demands concentration and deliberation and bridges the generation gap because **age doesn't come into angling talk.** Fishing is a social good and organising those competitions under guidance is part of it.

The gurus of a cruelty-free world, like the afore-mentioned Professor Linzey, equate hunting with rape, child abuse and torture. Professor Drewermann, a most influential German theologian, goes even further (*Der Spiegel*, no. 52, January 1998):

... biologically and morally correct it is to say that somebody who pulls a fish out of the water is causing more pain and death than a doctor performing an abortion in the third month.

I wonder what "more death" means exactly: are there degrees of death? The animal-rights people, are in influential positions right at the top everywhere. Animal rights from above, Bambi and Beatrix Potter from below: if this goes on unchallenged over another decade we'll reel in forever. That's why those "crackpot" ideas from the ivory towers of academia are so dangerous, and that's why Bill and you should be able to recognise them – knowing your enemy is half the battle.

Involvement in the widest sense means to participate in activities which counter those specious animal-rights ideas and promote positive thinking about angling. Local initiative is important and there are thousands of superb examples of involvement: cleaning streams, spending the day at the river with the disabled, organising an introductory course on aquatic life, instituting a year of the perch, collecting for a charity and so on. Over and above such activities, anglers must seek political influence and coordinate their efforts. I can't be more specific than that, but wherever anglers are united and influential, animal-rights pressure can be contained and that will mean less meddling with angling in the sense of imposed restrictions. Regarding the latter, Germany is the front runner in terms of rules and regulations which lead in only one direction: a complete ban. In the present social and political climate, complacency is a luxury anglers can't afford.

186

FISH MUST SWIM THREE TIMES

A thousand and one things in a thousand and one different shades and guises converge on the angler and the bait at the end of his line. Time, place, tackle, conditions (light, rain, wind, etc.) all play their role and so do experience, reason, tradition, mood and knowledge. It's a dynamic process fusing intentions and imponderables into a unique yet universal experience which, if conditions are right, gives you a glimpse of perfection and, of course, a fish.

What about the culinary angle? After all, food is at the origins of angling. Remember our caveman? Just as he had

moments of reflection, he also must have had moments of culinary delight in the sense that he enjoyed his food beyond the mere filling of his stomach. He most certainly also had preferences: trout were easier to eat than bream. The bone situation hasn't changed since then. The point is that human hunting and eating are distinguished from animal hunting and eating because there is a reflective and appreciative side to them which animals lack. If it weren't for reflection and appreciation, we would still be sitting around the fire in the cave. It's easy to see the reflective side but appreciation? Just imagine the wild strawberries (any kind of sweet berry) back then: I am most certain that people were full of happy anticipation as the season for them drew closer. The savouring of that first berry was an appreciation, and there must have been moments when the caveman said to himself that this year's berries were even better than last year's and then connected that fact to, for example, the weather.

Be that as it may, the trout, perch and pike etc. are still the same as they were back then, and couldn't it be that those who like their fish best from the open fire like it so much because they share an authentic time-honoured smell and taste experience? The culinary experience of fish prepared over an open fire or wrapped in leaves in the embers, then as now, would roughly be the same. The sensation is an echo from a distant past. With this I wish to draw your attention to two points: The first one is that, as I mentioned at the beginning, angling has a pedigree like no other sport and the culinary angle confirms that. The second is that the gourmet side of angling is yet another of those contributing factors merging into the beauty of angling. It's not a necessary contributor: fishing can be enjoyed without its culinary delights, but with them the experience is, in my view, complete.

The art of catching fish has been described and analysed a million times over, the art of cooking fish perhaps a hundred thousand times over. But have you ever read an account of the art of eating fish? The art of eating fish? Yes, there is more to eating, especially eating fish, than perfunctory acts of mastication and gulping down the pulp. What I have in mind here are not the findings and subsequent terrorism of dietetics or – worse – cruelty-free food, nor the blinding blah-blah of Michelin experts and lifestyle gourmets, but rather the simple ability to appreciate and enjoy food and drink. As in all things there's a healthy balance somewhere between the mindless devourer and the sophisticated gourmet glutton.

A.A. Luce, author of one of the most important books on angling, *Fishing and Thinking*, feared that the title would be satirised and mocked as "Fishing and Drinking". Fishing and drinking: is there a problem? There is currently all over Europe "great concern" about drug and alcohol abuse among young people. Alcohol is blamed for almost any sort of trouble relating to young people (violence, crime etc.) and the causes for European-wide youth alcoholism are "rapid social and economic transition, civil conflict, poverty, homelessness and isolation " (www.who.dk). I am sure you notice that all these are extrinsic causes and that none are the individual agents' fault. The picture painted by certain politicians of European youth is one of a malleable mass of individuals without a will. On the basis of that assumption, all sorts of studies and recommendations are produced and policies implemented from which only one group of people profits: the concerned politicians and swarms of deeply concerned civil servants, social scientists and other hangers-on whose livelihood depends on issues. I haven't read a report yet which says, " Young people drink excessively because as individuals they don't know what's right or wrong any more because they have never been told what is right or wrong. The reason for this is that a completely misguided and irresponsible academic and political elite from the Seventies onward has attempted to systematically destroy the traditional web of values which are a guide for the individual and the cement of society." Besides, is the alcohol problem really as bad as we are led to believe? The original question was: Fishing and drinking: is there a problem? The answer is: in excess yes, in moderation no. And for perspective let me add the following lines from Bert L. Vallee M.D. (*Scientific American* June 1998):

In the context of contaminated water supply, ethyl alcohol may indeed have been mother's milk to a nascent Western civilization. Beer and wine were free of pathogens. And the antiseptic power of alcohol, as well as the natural acidity of wine and beer, killed many pathogens when the alcoholic drinks were diluted with the sullied water supply. Dating from the taming and conscious application of the fermentation process, people of all ages in the West have therefore consumed beer and wine, not water, as their major daily thirst quenchers. Babylonian clay tablets more than 6000 years old give beer recipes, complete with illustrations. The Greek term akratidzomai which came to mean "to breakfast," literally translates as "to drink undiluted wine." Breakfast apparently could include wine as a bread dip, and "bread and beer" connoted basic necessity much as does today's expression "bread and butter."

The experience in the East differed greatly. For at least the past 2000 years, the practice of boiling water, usually for tea, has created a potable supply of nonalcoholic beverages. In addition, genetics played an important role in making Asia avoid alcohol: approximately half of all Asian people lack an enzyme necessary for complete alcohol metabolism, making the experience of drinking quite unpleasant. Thus, beer and wine took their place as staples only in Western societies and remained there until the end of the last century...

Humanity at any moment of history is inevitably caught in that time, as trapped as an insect in amber. The mores, traditions and

190

attitudes of an era inform the individuals then living, often blinding them to the consideration of alternatives. Alcohol today is a substance primarily of relaxation, celebration and, tragically, mass destruction. To consider it as having been a primary agent for the development of an entire culture may be jolting, even offensive, to some. Any good physician, however, takes a history before attempting a cure.

Several questions come immediately to mind: are alcohol-free societies non-violent societies? Are alcohol-free societies happier societies? Are alcohol-free societies drug-free societies? Are alcohol-free societies free societies? The final word on fishing and drinking must go to Izaak Walton's:

Let's go merrily to supper, and then have a gentle touch at singing and drinking; but the last with moderation.

Eating the fish you catch is for celebration, for pleasure, for partying. But just as there is no necessity to drink alcohol today, there is no necessity to eat the fish you catch. The spell of necessity can be cast over a great many objects, activities and sources of pleasure: Is football a necessity? Is golf a necessity? Is fishing a necessity? Is music a necessity? Is television a necessity? Is eating sausages a necessity? Is Coke a necessity? Is cutlery a necessity? Is collecting stamps a necessity? Is playing cards a necessity? Is the internet a necessity? In fact, if you rationalise and reduce, you'll find that you can easily consign mankind back to Stone Age when we lived and survived on bare necessities. There are only a few real necessities and if man had stuck to them there would have been no progress at all. Aiming for the unnecessary is what advanced man. At the basis of progress, and of culture, then as now, is leisure – because leisure opens the mind for reflection and speculation. No leisure, no culture, no progress.

If you catch, cook and eat a fish, you might be tempted to rationalise this in the functional terms of the food-chain. But that, you'll surely agree, is only a fraction of the story because the fish in question is not just any fish. It is your fish. By catching it, it doesn't merely become lawfully yours. It's more than that: a gift, maybe, a reward for your toils, or both. It's nature's way of smiling on you. This is not an entirely new idea: Walton frequently quotes the 16th-century naturalist Aldrovandus:

Aldrovandus says the salmon, the grayling, and trout and all fish that live in clear and sharp streams, are made by mother nature of such exact shape and pleasant colours purposely to invite us to a joy and contentedness in feasting with her.

Walton cautiously adds:

Whether this is a truth or not is not my purpose to dispute;

The biggest smile comes when a salmon, after its incredible travels and adventures, falls for your fly. When you eat that salmon, perhaps with friends, it's like the last piece of a puzzle falling into place: the communion with nature, with Creation, is perfect. **Cooking and eating the fish you catch is part of the beauty of angling.** Fish preparation and cooking automatically pulls you irresistibly into yet another world: the culture of cooking. Just think of the things you have to know when preparing a simple fish dish like trout fillet in butter with potatoes. You need to master the art

of filleting (What knife? How?), choosing the right butter, the right potatoes and you want a sprinkling of chives also. But there is more to it: how much heat on the butter, skin side or meat side down first? How long, how do I turn it, what's the right wine to wash it down and so on. As in all other areas of angling you'll require knowledge, reason, skills and virtues. And in cooking, too, the tradition and communication angle comes into play: there's a knowledge transfer and there's lots of fun in the kitchen. And in much the same way as there is convergence of all your skills and hopes pinned on the bait trying to attract a fish, there is convergence of all the elements of your achievement on the plate with your catch.

By learning to prepare, cook and serve fish or, at least, by looking over the shoulder of somebody who does, you begin to acquire the ability to appreciate food and drink. Even if you find that you don't enjoy cooking or have no talent for it, you'll have an idea of what's involved and what's happening and that cooking is a craft and not an industry. Not so long ago it would have been unthinkable not to sit down for a meal, whereas nowadays it's quite common to lunch while walking, which might be just as well because what you stuff down your throat might not be worth sitting down for. Knowledge about cooking entails a change in the way you eat: you'll appreciate the chef's (your mother's or whoever cooks) work and the quality and source of your food.

The Compleat Angler is peppered with references to the preparation and cooking of different kinds of fish and their respective culinary merits. The perch is a "dainty dish" the tench "eats pleasantly" and the pike, if done as Walton suggests, is a great delicacy:

> *This dish of meat is too good for any but anglers, or very honest men; and I trust you will prove both, and therefore have trusted you with this secret. [The recipe]*

I can't presently recall that any of my giants of angling literature has enquired deeply into the culinary aspects. There is, for example, no culinary competence in A.A. Luce; and Hugh Falkus's culinary recommendations in *Sea Trout Fishing* are recipes for disaster. You'll find the poor sea trout in the company of bacon and mushrooms or, worse still, both. You shouldn't even show bacon to a sea trout. A

194

fresh-run sea trout is so delicate a fish of such exquisite and subtle taste that you could eat it raw. The cooking of it should underline and, at best, enhance its taste and not divert from it or even cover it. "Ah, but there's no disputing over taste", you might object. What is in this well-worn adage in regard to cooking? The following are but a few tentative casts: Man is an omnivore, man eats everything and can enjoy almost anything. Of the Chinese it is said that they eat anything but submarines. Newly born mice dipped in a honey sauce was considered a delicacy in ancient Rome. "Ugh"? But where essentially is the difference between that and oyster slurping?

The point is that many tastes are acquired (like whisky, wine and smoking) accompanied by a lot of intention, determination and imagination to discover and savour culinary delights. The human search for food is aimed primarily at satisfying a need, but the very moment that need is satisfied the search for more starts. More sensation, more experience, more variety, more refinement – and this drive for refinement in culinary matters is common to all societies past and present.

Walton's culinary recommendations show two things: in an age when food security was science fiction, no source of nourishment could be disregarded. More important, however, is the point that without culinary culture no angler is a "compleat" angler. Walton's recipes might not conform to our refined present-day ideas of cooking fish, but that doesn't in any way touch the fact that cooking and enjoying fish are an integral part of angling. And while I am at it, I might as well take up the cudgels on Walton's behalf in another respect: his technical advice has been more than frowned upon, and the prose it's couched in has been criticised as long-winded and belittled as quaint. The style we can overlook here: but the message is that the angler must take great care over his tactics, i.e. his preparation and approach and the exercise of his skills. Breeding worms, baking boilies and tying flies must not be left to chance if you want to be successful. Walton's advice might be outdated, but his message is the same as that of any modern detailed manual on how to go about something! But back to the culinary angle: "This dish of meat is too good for any but anglers". Only too right: those ignorant non-anglers who can't appreciate the work involved in honestly catching a fish don't deserve ambrosia. And by the same token, those chefs reducing

potential delight to mere food should serve a turn in purgatory.

A couple of years ago my rod pointed to Cumbria's Lake District for fishing and for Wordsworth. We (our friends Rosalind and Paul, and Regina and myself) stayed at a hotel in the Maryport region. The lobby sported, encouragingly, a 19th century angling scene featuring a little girl fishing a pond. The wiring of the hotel was also positively 19th century. If you switched on the light in your room, you could hear the electricity sizzle through the cables and flexes. We were accommodated on the top floor. The loft above us was a nature reserve: neither the roof nor the loft had been interfered with for centuries. This was late spring, so the loft was still busy, and the smell of guano permeated through the ceiling. Meanwhile, our friends' room below us took the smoke and conversation from the lounge below them. You could certainly say the hotel had atmosphere.

For fishing I went on the very first day near Cleator Moor where I met a friendly fellow angler assuring me that the local rainbow trout were of superior quality, in fact the very best in the world. I was lucky and got two fine trout which I thought would make a lovely dinner. The girl at the reception desk looked slightly aghast and went "ugh" when I handed her the bag with the two trout. I asked her to hand them into the kitchen, that they were our dinner and that they were so fresh they were still almost alive. At this, positive disgust showed on an otherwise pretty face. The staff of the hotel, I should add, were all on the teenage – if not adolescent – side and (I noticed with approval) all locally recruited. The girl went on her trouty errand to the kitchen and I to our quarters. Opening the door was quite a job: you had to turn the knob and then give the door a really hard shove, aiming to keep your balance so as not to fall into the room.

Anyway, I managed and I hadn't even slammed the door back into its frame when the phone rang. It was the receptionist explaining to me in the sweetest of voices that the trout couldn't be done for dinner nor at any other time, as this would not be in accord with the food regulations governing hotels in England. They were terribly sorry and so on. This left me temporarily speechless. Before my mind's eye I already could see cats, foxes and martens fighting in the backyard over my two beauties. I insisted that I was only half an idiot and that

I had specifically enquired (which was the case) before we booked whether the chef would cook the trout, if I were indeed to catch any, and that the manager had agreed. "Check with the manager, please," I said and intimidated her further with an unnecessarily rude comment about trying to fool me with food regulations. Poor girl. She was back on the phone half an hour later and informed me that we could have the trout for dinner.

Once upon a time, the expensive and luxurious garden furniture of the dining room must have been the pride of the owners. Now, it was genuinely antique – the cobwebs testified to it. It wasn't exactly a confidence-inspiring ambience. Nevertheless, the trout it had to be, there and then and nowhere else. The father of the girl who took our order must have been a drill sergeant in the army. She was a solid figure fixing each of us in turn with a mixture of suspicion and contempt and then barking at all of us, "Areyerrrreadytooorrrder!". Sitting up straight we ordered just the main course which would be trout, potatoes and vegetables and a bottle of Chablis. While the waitress clumped through a swinging door into the kitchen shouting orders (or did I hear it "bloody foreigners, bloody trout"? Surely not!) at the chef, we looked at each other and around us. We were the only guests – the restaurant didn't seem over-popular. Before we could share our concern yet another girl, hardly sixteen, dressed up more for the disco than for waiting turned up with the Chablis. "That's efficient," I thought but revised my premature praise when I had to fish out my Swiss army knife from my pocket and open the bottle myself. The disco queen couldn't find the corkscrew and even if she had found it, she probably wouldn't have known how to use it. Greatly relieved that the problem was solved, she hopped off, not to be seen again that evening.

Now that Chablis was absolutely out of this world: never before (and never since) had any of us tasted anything like it. Extraordinary. And if I told you the price, you wouldn't believe me. The only explanation I have for what they charged is that that Chablis must have fallen off the back of a lorry and nobody knew what value to pin on it. The wine changed our mood considerably and with great expectations we looked forward to the trout. Savouring that Chablis, letting it roll around the tongue, Paul ventured, "We could be in for a treat here". He could have been right: it sometimes happens that places don't look the part and then turn out to be veritable gourmet temples. We were in for a treat indeed: the trout were served in the still closed tin foil on a huge plate. Opening the tin foil, we saw the two beautiful but hopelessly overdone, soggy trout. On top of that they weren't properly gutted. To this day I fail to comprehend how the "chef" managed to get them to that absolute sogginess.

We managed to salvage parts by drying them on paper napkins procured from a sideboard. The vegetables were boiled potatoes, chips, mashed potatoes and peas. The peas were delicious: just the right amount of preservatives and taste-enhancing chemicals in them – they actually tasted like peas. We ordered a second bottle of Chablis. It was the most awfully cooked trout we had ever eaten and the best wine we had ever drunk. Incidentally, the convention that it's got to be white wine with fish dates back to the French kings Louis XIV–Louis XVI. Why it's got to be wine (white or red) and not water would lead too far from our present topic. But do you think there would be as much passionate writing about wine if there were no alcohol in it?

We decided to ignore the shortcomings of the hotel and stayed on (the Chablis tilted the scales and there was also a Port, obviously from the same lorry). The next two days we followed Wordsworth's tracks, dining elsewhere and then I went fishing again. Same place and again two trout. The girl at the reception desk took them with a conspiratorial smile, which I didn't know how to interpret. She listened politely when I told her, equally politely, that the last time they had been overdone. Come dinner time, we all met at the bar for a drink and when the drill sergeant roared at us: "Yourrtablleisrready!" we made our way to the dining room and obediently trooped to the assigned table.

In no time the disco queen appeared with the Chablis and to relieve her obvious embarrassment (again no corkscrew) I opened it again. In "exchange", I asked for a bucket of ice. "Bucket of ice?" she looked at me as if I were an extraterrestrial. "What for?" she couldn't help herself asking. After we got the bucket and secured another bottle, she disappeared again to disco or wherever. Shortly afterwards the trout arrived. Surprise, surprise! They were properly filleted for the four of us, the potatoes and vegetables were nicely arranged and the

trout were good. Not perfect, but plain honest good, and as the trout were of exceptional quality, it was an exceptional meal. It was great and we happily ate and left the table in the best of moods.

On the last day before we went out (ladies for a stroll on the beach, Paul for a walk and myself for fishing), the girl at the reception desk informed us that that day was a special day and that we could have dinner only between six and eight. Why, was the obvious question. The answer was that there would be a concert by a famous singer-songwriter in the public bar which would start at 8.30pm and that the staff were needed there. Okay. We enjoyed trout and Chablis between six and eight, and Rosalind and Regina decided to attend the concert of that famous singer-songwriter. Paul and I opted for the dusty lounge and the fabulous port.

After about an hour Rosalind and Regina joined us, and we asked how the concert had been. We learnt that Rosalind and Regina were the only audience apart from the hotel staff up until the interval and that the hotel staff enjoyed the show tremendously. The staff consisted of: the receptionist, the barman, the chef, the drill sergeant, the disco queen, the chamber maid and the handyman. The concert might have been advertised but was purely and solely put on as entertainment for the hotel staff. And before the concert started, our lady detectives learned that the chef had been away on the day of the soggy trout and that the handyman had been in charge of the kitchen. He had had two ready-made menus there but the trout threw him off balance.

That explained the food regulation gambit. For the trout recipe one of the girls had phoned back home, but the instructions had clearly not been sufficient. These young people were kind, willing, helpful, honest and eager to do things right. But how could they succeed without somebody experienced telling them? Well, in any case the youngsters were likeable, the fishing was good, the trout (after the first) excellent and the Chablis and the port fantastic, but we won't go there again: something, somehow, was not right, but that was certainly not the young people's fault. I certainly would object to sending the handyman to purgatory on account of his soggy trout.

The golden, time-honoured rule of cooking fish is, that they must swim three times: in water, in butter and in wine. This probably sends a light shudder down ten out of ten Japanese backs. Closer scrutiny of the TST (three swims theory) does however reveal that the prejudice is ill- founded. Point one: fish must swim in water. Water means clean water, healthy water: a healthy aquatic environment gives us top-quality fish. There's nothing in this to which Japanese (or any other) fish connoisseurs could possibly object.

The other day I was fishing on the river Aare in the small tourist town of Interlaken, Switzerland, a favourite with Japanese tourists as a base from which to explore the Bernese Oberland. I was there very early in the morning because the promenade there gets busy later on and early morning is the most promising time for grayling. I was fishing, fully concentrated, and it was only when I reeled in to change the nymph that I noticed four people behind me. They were two Japanese couples who bowed politely when I said "hello", making me feel like a proper boor. **I am sure Japanese anglers can gracefully bow with rod in hand.** "What fish?"

one of the men whispered politely. "Grayling," I whispered back. I could see they didn't know the word. "Trout," I ventured. They all smiled, which I took as a sign that they had understood. I also interpreted it to the effect that I could go on fishing without being rude. I continued fishing, but the concentration was gone because I could feel them still standing behind me watching. So after a while I reeled in once more to change nymphs, and there they stood like statues smiling at me. I smiled back, from which the speaker of the group probably inferred that he was allowed to talk. "Eat trout?" to which I answered, "Yes, eat trout, trout very good!" "Trout very good," the speaker repeated and then said something to the others, upon which they all nodded appreciatively, bowed again and then dissolved away as silently as they had come.

I wonder now what they would say to point two: swimming in butter doesn't mean drowning in butter. Cooking trout, which I know best, is a delicate operation. Here's my rundown: just a little dab of butter in the frying pan will do – excess butter kills the trout. Then heat the butter so that it just bubbles but doesn't turn brown; lightly fry the fillets on both sides and then put them on a dish which you have covered with kitchen foil. You then put the trout in the pre-heated oven leave it there for a while and take it out when the flesh is still rare to medium. Drain off the excess butter in a little bowl and put the fillets on the plates. Add a little salt and chives and serve with potatoes.

This simple way of cooking trout can be used also for salmon steaks. If the trout and the salmon are fresh and of superior quality, anything more than that is overdone – the trout or salmon will by itself taste delicious, its taste only enhanced by a little butter, salt and chives.

No professional chef dares to cook as simply as that because then he is not seen to be cooking (concocting some complicated and sophisticated recipe) and won't win awards, points or stars. Is this simple European way (poaching is another superb method) of cooking trout or salmon that far off sushi? The idea is basically the same: keep the taste of the fish as pronounced as possible (and incidental to that, keep its full nutritional value) by doing as little to it as possible. There is with sushi soy sauce and horseradish, which corresponds

to the butter, salt and chives. I don't think that little bit of butter would unduly upset Japanese stomachs which brings me to sake and wine. Again, swimming doesn't mean drowning, but I don't mind if the fish has plenty to swim about in the third time round. Judging from my admittedly limited experience of Japanese restaurants, the Japanese also like to give their fish plenty of swimming freedom in their stomachs. I wonder what Walton would have made of sushi? One thing is for certain: he would have preferred sushi to fish fingers because fish fingers are barbaric, sushi is culture and so are trout, salmon and other fish, the European way. To catch a fish sportingly, to prepare it, to cook it and to serve it, is culture.

THE SPIRIT OF LUTRY

Beauty, you'll remember, is not just the sum of certain qualities but rather their unity. That unity is a glimpse of perfection and is different from the mere sum. Part of the beauty of angling is its challenging diversity. The very complexity and depth of angling makes it the king of sports. I shall now try to sum up the various areas of angling we have touched on. The listing suggests a neatness and completeness that isn't there. All the areas of interest overlap and are interdependent.

Nature

Angling takes place in nature. Obvious? Yes and no. If by "nature" you mean the totality of the physical world, then yes, of course angling takes place in nature. Obvious. In that sense, everything takes place in nature: football and computer chess take place in nature. What I mean by nature here is the countryside in the widest sense, in contrast to a controlled environment such as a football stadium. Not so obvious, because you could just as well argue that the countryside is also a controlled environment shaped by the needs and activities of human beings. Even Scotland's highland wilderness was man-made through the clearances and the subsequent introduction of sheep. The landscape is a sheepscape, so to speak. Likewise, most of the pre-alpine and alpine landscape in Switzerland, although natural-looking, was man-made through cattle farming. Cowscape, so to speak.

The nature I speak of in the context of angling can range from the urban pond to the complete wilderness of a lake deep in the Canadian forests. In that range lies another of the truly unique features of angling: No other pursuit allows you to plug in everywhere to nature. There is no network so complete as that of angling possibilities (i.e. water), which is why angling has taken root in all human cultures

207

the world over. Angling unites the most diverse traditions in the sense that it is seen as a good. Angling is a common good and there is common wisdom about angling transcending language barriers and all.

Angling is applied natural history and natural science. In order to be successful, you need to be able to read in the book of natural history. A successful angler shows a lively interest in his angling environment and tries to analyse what happens there and how it bears on his angling. The questions to which you might want answers range from the simple to the complex: What do low-flying swallows mean? Why is it chub don't take during the time of elder-tree blossom? To find answers, more often than not you have to call in the auxiliaries: ichthyology (the science of fish), entomology (the science of insects), meteorology (the science of weather) and geology (the science of rocks). Chemistry, physics and mathematics also often play their part. The auxiliaries open windows and views that no other sport can open. By studying insects, for example, anglers look into a microcosm full of beauty and wonders. This world and many others are part and parcel of angling. Can you think of any other sport the nature of which even remotely involves such breadth?

Knowledge

From the study of nature and natural science the angler gains knowledge. The other, perhaps more important, source of knowledge is the knowledge transferred from the experienced to the inexperienced, from the old angler to the young angler. Angling bridges generation gaps because it unites in purpose the most diverse people of all ages. By receiving knowledge and by questioning and discussing it, the young angler acquires social skills and learns about rules and their meaning. This is the principal reason why angling "keeps the boys off the streets". Angling knowledge is not confined to angling in the way that tennis knowledge is confined to tennis. Tennis knowledge does not really invite reflection, whereas angling knowledge positively provokes it. Moreover, angling knowledge is not a static body of rules and references (as in chess) but a dynamic process. Angling knowledge, in the final analysis, is knowledge about life.

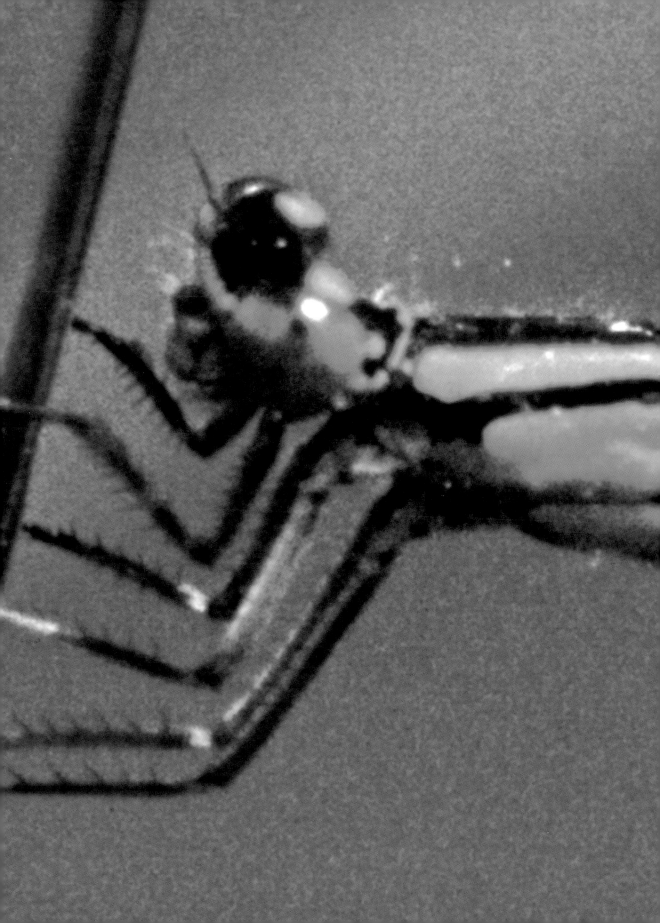

Practical reason

If you want to win a tennis match, you need skill, stamina and psychology, but to bash a tennis ball about you don't need complex deliberation. In angling it is different. There you have to proceed systematically to get your fish. Regardless of what you fish for or whether you fish with worm or fly, before you begin you have to take various elements into account: the weather conditions, the time of day, the water level, the water temperature, the strength of your cast and the nature of your prey to mention but a few. Preparation for even "I'll nip just down the river for an hour" requires some clear thinking in order to enhance the chances of success. Fishing, like no other sport, is governed by knowledge and reason. True, you also need skills, but these are without value if your reasoning isn't sound. Angling is the most logical sport there is. Again, can you think of any other sport or pastime of which this can be said?

Virtues

Angling leads you to prudence, patience and moderation because you catch more fish by being virtuous. The immoderate angler who drinks excessively and goes fishing with a king-size hangover diminishes his pleasure by feeling sick and will therefore miss fish after fish. Virtuousness in this respect and others increases pleasure. The pleasure, the satisfaction and the contentment generated by a successful angling day can't be matched by accountancy-oriented sports such as tennis. Again, can you tell me of a sport which pivots around virtues?

Skills

The skills involved in angling are incredibly diverse. There's knotting to begin with, which is a science in itself. Then there is casting – all kinds of casting, from the handline to the double-hander. Then there are boilie baking, worm breeding and flytying. If you regularly fish from a boat you learn about oarwork or engines. If you fish mountain lakes and stay overnight, you will need to know about putting up your tent or rough-sleeping. There are innumerable skills involved in angling – again, compare that range with other sports or pastimes and you'll find that angling has no equal.

Reflection

All anglers at some moment sit back and reflect. Angling entails philosophy and poetry. "Angling is somewhat like poetry, men are to be born so," as Walton says. There is inquisitive reflection on down-to-earth questions such as why the fish don't take, and then there are the more philosophical reflections on, say, the "injustice" of your trying hard and right and catching nothing and another angler, doing it all wrong has success. Angling typically inspires poetry, of which it is said that when philosophy is at the end of its tether, poetry takes over. Again, do you know of any other sport or pastime which offers "inbuilt" philosophy and poetry or perhaps even glimpses of wisdom?

"Angling is somewhat like poetry, men are to be born so." Does this mean that there are approx. 4 million poets in the United Kingdom? Just as there are people who simply don't care about poetry there are people with a very weak disposition to fish. To them fishing (and poetry) is so remote they don't even know it's there. Then there are those who try but remain indifferent to the experience. The third group takes up angling but then drops it again, because some other overriding interest appears on the scene. The most important group is that which tries and then starts to think fishing.

For born anglers, fishing then takes centre stage. However, a born angler doesn't necessarily go fishing all the time. My fishing biography resembles that of most of my fishing friends. We all started fishing as boys and at some stage as young adults we got caught up in our jobs, troubles, careers, marriages and families, which absorbed all our energy until the moment when angling made a comeback. Such comebacks can be brought about by many different causes but the effect is the same: if fishing is taken up again after a pause – sometimes of years – it usually gets hold of the angler stronger than ever before. That is the moment when the angler tries to gear his life more towards his angling.

To say "angling is somewhat like poetry" does not mean that the one is an instance of the other. It just means that there are similarities: both the angler and the poet require, for example, some of the same talents. Creativity is one of them. Telling the story of the one that got away is a creative achievement, just like a poem about a sunset. As in any other field, there are people who will be particularly good at it. The one will be a celebrated angler and the other a poet laureate. Poet and angler share other concerns. Take the weather. Poet and angler, on occasion, pray for rain while the rest of mankind is happy with bright, sunny weather: the poet to get into that inspired, melancholic mood when the rain taps on the window; the angler because the river needs water so that the salmon start to run. While the angler keeps worms in the fridge, the poet might keep rotten apples in his desk drawer. It is reported of the famous German poet Schiller that he did exactly that, for he couldn't work without the smell of rotten apples.

The power that fishing wields over the angler (or poetry over the poet) is such that he can't escape it, and in that sense angling (and poetry) is likened to an addiction. That aspect of angling has been highlighted by Robert Travers (quoted from Bryn Hammond, *Halcyon Days*):

The true trout fisherman is like a drug addict; he dwells in a tight little dream world of his own, and the men about him, whom he observes obliviously spending their days pursuing money and power, genuinely puzzle him, as he doubtless does them. He prides himself on being an unbribed soul. So he is by way of being a philosopher, too, and sometimes he fishes not because he regards fishing as being so terribly important but because he suspects that so many of the other concerns of men are equally unimportant. Under his smiling coat of tan there often lurks a layer of melancholy and disillusion, a quiet awareness – and acceptance – of the fugitive quality of man and all his enterprises. If he must chase a will-o'-the-wisp, he prefers that it be a trout. And so the fisherman fishes. It is an act of humility and a small rebellion. And it is something more. To him fishing is an island of reality in a world of dream and shadow.

I don't go along with the sombre note in this; the beauty of angling is bright and positive. Besides, I don't quite agree that a distinguishing feature of a fisherman is that he is like a drug addict. On the contrary, the true fisherman escapes the temptation of addiction. Becoming an addicted angler is easy, but you want to become a good angler and I don't think you can divide reality as suggested in the last sentence. Travers wrote in *Testament of a Fisherman* (quoted from Bryn Hammond, *Halcyon Days*):

I fish because I love to; because I love the environs where trout are found, which are invariably beautiful and hate the environs where crowds of people are found, which are invariably ugly...

Now that's a different note altogether, involving notions of love and beauty. I prefer it to the drug-addict comparison, which somehow unnecessarily lowers the status of the angler.

The reason the angler and the poet are socially accepted, despite their somewhat non-conformist existence, is that now and then they come up with the goodies. Nothing is more convincing than a beautiful fish or a beautiful poem. There is undeniably something radical about angler and poet. The radical aspect surfaces the moment your daughter brings home the young man she wants to marry. Not too many parents will be overjoyed to hear from their prospective son-in-law that what he does in life is catch fish or write poetry (or, worse still, both). Even successful anglers and poets are frowned upon, as the poet Alexander Pope certainly experienced:

Sir, I admit your general rule
That every poet is a fool:
But you yourself may serve to show it,
That every fool is not a poet.

It's quite clear, I think, that Walton's angler-poet analogy can be substantiated. The answer to the question whether there are 4 million poets in the United Kingdom therefore is: potentially yes, and they seek inspiration by going fishing. Apart from being potential poets, who are they, the anglers? For many sports you could easily make a profile of the typical participant in terms of education, social background and income: this can't be done for angling. Anglers the world over are drawn from all walks of life – no other sport or pastime features such diversity. Whereas I could imagine a sociology of certain types of angling, it is difficult to see how that could be done for all angling. Angling and anglers defy compartmentalisation, and yet it has been tried.

The tangle theorist McGillicuddy, for one, attempted a tentative typology of anglers and their style. Although derived from lifelong observation of fly fisherman, his findings could probably be applied to all the different methods of angling. In his long angling life McGillicuddy noticed that the more advanced an angler's career in terms of age and experience, the more he resembles one of the fish-eating birds of his angling environment. Here are three examples from his notes (paraphrased) to show you what this is all about:

The heron-angler

Self-importance and an inflated ego on stilts. This bird knows there is something perfect about it. The heron could be a private secretary or an accountant. He is fully aware of the exaggerated meticulousness of his proceedings and easily offended if he feels that you don't take him seriously. Next time you watch a heron, just think something unkind about him and before long he will have read your thoughts and fly off, punishing you with an indignant look. Nonetheless, it's hard to ignore the beautiful purposefulness and precision in the heron's stalk.

Anglers of this type approach their sport in a systematic way with as little as possible left to chance. The flies they tie conform to the tying instructions to the letter and their neatness has no equivalent in nature. They are lined up in the fly box like soldiers on parade. The heron-angler has to steer himself to take a fly out of his box because it breaks up the geometry.

The dipper-angler

The dipper is a jovial fellow and could in real life be a vegetable wholesale trader. Just as the dipper hops or flies from stone to stone to see what's on offer, the vegetable wholesale trader goes from stall to stall to see what's on offer. While the heron smiles grimly, the dipper smiles brightly. The dipper doesn't mind company and is always ready for a good joke. He dives with so much pleasure that one is tempted to think he does it just for the sake of it. Dipper-anglers approach their business a bit offhand. They are not given to racking their brains on how to proceed before they start fishing. They simply give it a whirl; they fish the spot and if there are no offers, they move on. Typically there are two of them together. They fish some distance apart, but once in a while they like to meet and chat about how they have been getting along. If they meet fellow anglers, they're helpful and generous. Their fly box would typically be a wild assortment of all sorts of flies: self-tied, bought ones and others given to them by colleagues.

The kingfisher-angler

The kingfisher could be the centre forward of a football team. He is the opportunist type: small, agile, almost invisible and always in the right place when it matters. The kingfisher- angler's approach is characterised by waiting and watching. He will analyse a likely spot until he knows it like the back of his hand. If he feels disturbed in scrutinising a likely spot, indignation gets the better of him and he goes elsewhere. It's not that he is not civil; it's just that he doesn't like to be disturbed. The kingfisher type is secretive, but it is clear from the way he goes about things that he is as systematic as the heron type. But whereas the heron type makes a dogma out of his approach, the kingfisher type is an opportunist. I don't know what the inside of a fly box of a kingfisher-type angler looks like, because I have never seen one. I suspect it's fairly neat and ordered along well-defined categories. The kingfisher would have none of the eclecticism of the dipper.

We don't need to follow McGillicuddy into all his analytical and descriptive depth, because the idea behind this typology is so

ingeniously simple that you can start yourself immediately (osprey, crested grebe, cormorant, etc.). It's quite fun, actually, to spot the bird in your fellow angler. I have my doubts about its accuracy and usefulness, though, because the types, personalities, individualities, approaches, attitudes and techniques in angling are so diverse that it seems impossible to classify them. There is, however, another message in McGillicuddy's exercise: it just shows how much the angler can blend in, plug in with nature.

To this day, for most people a boat with an angler symbolises peace and calm. A windsurfer certainly doesn't. Why? The answer must lie in the fact that the angler communes with nature, whereas the windsurfer somehow seems to impose himself. The angler strikes the observer as natural, as belonging there, while the windsurfer, with his glaring fluorescent sail, really is a blot on the lake in the sense that he doesn't convey tranquillity at all. The windsurfer certainly is not an aesthetic asset to a lone lake. The windsurfer is a transitory figure while the fisherman in communion with nature is for real and forever.

That sounds mildly vague and wildly romantic – what exactly does it mean? Am I not merely painting another picture, like Poussin did, using the angler to add a symbolic touch emphasising tranquillity? If Poussin or I wanted to emphasise or symbolise tranquillity, why put the angler there in the first place? Wouldn't an idyllic lake scene be even more peaceful without the angler? No, because the angler belongs there, he's meant to be there. Ever since the first man dangled his baited hook to a fish, anglers have been part of all kinds of waterscapes.

This certainly isn't the case with our windsurfer. A psychologist would perhaps say that the angler is part of the collective subconscious whereas the windsurfer isn't. The windsurfer will probably never in a million years ingrain himself in the public mind like the angler. Windsurfing is all about lifestyle, entertainment, thrills – and so is angling, you might object. True, there are lifestyle, entertainment and thrills in angling but there is more to it than that. Fishing is a human gesture signalling the joyful acceptance and understanding of the terms and conditions of Creation. The materialist and Darwinist would say the angler is no more than an example of successful

222

adaptation. That opinion is accurate but doesn't cover the whole ground. Catching fish with hook and line symbolises like nothing else the duality in the human condition in relation to nature: we're attached and detached at the same time. The boat with the angler illustrates this. The reason why the non-angler perceives boat and angler as an image of tranquillity is that, in the order of things, he is in the right place where he is. The observer recognises an objective harmony in reality.

The angler is in harmony with nature: he is in communion with it. This communion doesn't come free: you have to do something. There might be born anglers, but even they have to learn, which brings us full circle back to tradition, i.e. the handing down of knowledge. Enlightened non-anglers (especially mothers of boys who go fishing) know that becoming an angler is a thorny path. There certainly are moments of glory but disappointments, frustrations and plain hard graft are part and parcel of the art and enjoyment of angling. Alright, but the sceptic might still question this "communion with nature" and insist on more: What is it precisely, this communion? There are two main strands.

Going fishing is an activity which can't be done piecemeal. Playing chess, for example, can be done piecemeal. If you play it on your computer, you can stop at any time and continue at any time you wish. Playing chess against the computer doesn't require interaction with anything other than the computer. Even if you interrupt your game of chess for a week, the game still makes sense. Fishing requires integrality. Your intention and equipment has to be complete (line, hook, bait and whatever else is needed), you have to know what you're doing, your timing has to be right, your choice of weapons has to be right and so on. Omitting or neglecting one of the major components or elements of angling will lead to disaster. Angling forces you to consider and to coordinate the most diverse elements and to master unforeseen complications. Chess with the computer on the other hand takes place in a fairly isolated arena, whereas angling takes place in real life.

Remember Baumgarten and "aesthetics is the science of sensory cognition"? The second strand of the communion is that in pursuit of fish, men – through the very proximity to nature and frequent

224

exposure to it – experience sensory cognition. Fishing in other words is an aesthetic experience. What does that mean exactly? In the internet I stumbled over a captivating article by Frederick Turner entitled *How Beauty Evolves* (www.dallasinstitute.org). In a passage there the author expresses with supreme clarity what the aesthetic experience is:

> *Aesthetic perception is not a vague and touchy-feely thing relative to ordinary perception; quite the reverse. This is why, given an infinite number of theories that will logically explain the facts,* **scientists will sensibly always choose the most beautiful theory.** *For good reason: this is the way the world works...*

...But this line of investigation has clearly brought us to a question which it seems audacious to ask in this anti-metaphysical age. Let us ask it anyway: what is the deepest tendency or theme of the universe?

The author then gives a tentative list about the "theme" of the universe:

1. Unity in multiplicity – the universe does seem to be one, though it is full of an enormous variety and quantity of things. Our best knowledge about its beginning, if it had one, is that everything in the universe was contracted into a single hot dense atom.

2. Complexity within simplicity: the universe is very complicated, yet it was generated by very simple physical laws.

3. Generativeness and creativity: the universe generates a new moment every moment, and each moment has genuine novelties. Its tendency or theme is that it should not just stop. As it cooled, it produced all the laws of chemistry, all the new species of animals and plants, and finally ourselves and our history.

4. Rhythmicity: the universe can be described as a gigantic, self-nested scale of vibrations, from the highest-frequency particles, which oscillate with an energy of ten milliontrillion giga-electron volts, to the slowest conceivable frequency (or the deepest of all notes), which vibrates over a period sufficient for a single wave to cross the entire universe and return. Out of these vibrations, often in the most delicate and elaborate mixtures or harmonies of tone, everything is made.

5. Symmetry: shapes and forms are repeated or mirrored in all physical structures, whether at the subatomic, the atomic, the crystalline, the chemical, the biological, or the anthropological levels of reality. And the more complex and delicate the symmetry, the more opportunities it presents for symmetry-breaking, the readjustment of the system towards a new equilibrium, and thus adaptation toward even more comprehensive symmetries.

6. Hierarchical organization: big pieces of the universe contain control, and depend on smaller pieces, and smaller pieces still, and so on.

7. Self-similarity: related to the hierarchical property is a marvellous property now being investigated by chaos theorists and fractal mathematicians: the smaller parts of the universe often resemble in shape and structure the larger parts of which they are components, and those larger parts in turn resemble the still larger systems that contain them.

When I showed this passage to Bill, he frowned and commented rather dryly, "I don't want to be in harmony with the 'theme' of the universe, I want to catch trout." "That's the same thing," I replied and indeed that is, what I believe to be the case. The aesthetic experience is an integral part of angling which is why every angler is subject to it. Subject to it? Yes, the aesthetic experience comes to the angler by virtue of angling. The intensity of this experience might vary, different individuals have different capacities for the experience but nevertheless it is present in all angling. Unless, of course, the angler is anaesthetised by drink or other means. The aesthetic experience doesn't come just like that. You have to make it happen. In order to catch fish the angler must "open up" and let himself be taken in by the fly, the float or whatever. The essence of this precondition is beautifully described in the following paragraphs by Ted Hughes:

... I fished in still water, with a float. As you know all a fisherman does is stare at his float for hours on end. I have spent hundreds and hundreds of hours staring at a float -- a dot of red or yellow the size of a lentil, ten yards away. Those of you who have never done it, might think it is a very drowsy pastime. It is anything but that.

All the little nagging impulses, that are normally distracting your mind, dissolve. They have to dissolve if you are to go on fishing. If they do not then you cannot settle down: you get bored and pack up in a bad temper. But once they have dissolved, you enter one of the orders of bliss.

Your whole being rests lightly on your float, but not drowsily: very alert, so that the least twitch of the float arrives like an electric shock. And you are not only watching the float. You are aware, in a horizonless and slightly mesmerised way, like listening to the double bass in orchestral music, of the fish below in the dark. At every moment your imagination is alarming itself with the size of the thing slowly leaving the weeds and approaching your bait. Or with the world of beauties down there, suspended in total ignorance of you. And the whole purpose of this concentrated excitement, in this arena of apprehension and unforeseeable events, is to bring up some lovely solid thing like living metal from a world where nothing exists but those inevitable facts which raise life out of nothing and return it to nothing.

228

So you see, fishing with a float is a sort of mental exercise in concentration on a small point, while at the same time letting your imagination work freely to collect everything that might concern that still point: in this case that still point is the float and the things that concern the float are all the fish you are busy imagining, (Poetry in the Making)

The communion with nature is the basis of the beauty of angling. This applies to the lone trout angler in the wilderness as well as to the perch angler on the busy pier in Lutry on the Lake of Geneva. Before heading there, let's take stock:

Taking stock

At the beginning we started off with this list of statements about the good of angling:

- Angling is a healthy outdoor pursuit
- Angling is relaxing
- Angling is a fascinating pastime
- Angling keeps the boys off the streets
- Angling satisfies an primitive need
- Angling is character-building
- Angling is fun
- Angling inspires the understanding of nature

This list can easily be objected to on the grounds that it is not complete. Any list with statements about the good of angling falls short of completeness because, in line with the nature of angling, there is always yet another angle you hadn't thought of. Angling is that kind of all- embracing pursuit, and what we have seen clearly en route to here is that the central theme of all angling, all conceivable aspects of angling, is beauty. Whichever angling topic you choose to inquire into, **you'll sooner or later discover beauty at the bottom of all angling matters.** Sometimes beauty is obvious, as in landscape; sometimes it's hidden, as in the chemistry of monofilament. So if you fortify the particular list opposite with the general findings we have obtained, you can give a fairly comprehensive answer to the question "what is good about angling?"

1. A perfect aesthetic experience

Angling is a perfect aesthetic experience. In communion with nature, the angler gets a glimpse of perfection. The aesthetic experience is that which underlies all angling, that which renders the susceptible person defenceless to the spell of angling. The cause of the often described compulsory or even addictive nature of angling is the aesthetic experience. The aesthetic experience makes you see beauty. It is the "more" of "there is more to fishing than catching fish".

2. A blueprint for the good life

No other pastime pushes the participant willy-nilly to reflection and contemplation about practical matters and questions beyond the day. The search and pursuit of fish is the search and pursuit of the good life. In this I follow Walton who says of angling that it

will prove to be so pleasant, that it will prove to be like virtue, a reward to itself.

In his foreword to *The Compleat Angler* Thomas McGuane concludes

... equitable Izaak Walton, by demonstrating how watchfulness and awe can be taken from within the natural world, has much to tell us – that is less about how to catch fish than about how to be thankful that we may catch fish. He tells us how to live.

Where there is angling, there is that blueprint for the good life lying ready. All you have to pick up your rod and go fishing.

3. The most universal university

Angling draws the angler deeper into the works of nature than any other pastime, and by doing so it involves him in the most diverse fields of inquiry. The range of subjects bearing on angling encompasses practically everything under the sun, because practically everything under the sun can, at some moment in time, be of vital importance to success in angling. The good angler will have an interest in the gigantic movements of celestial bodies (moon phases) as well as the microscopic universe of the protozoa. Course work, so to speak, is practical and with an end in view (catching a fish or catching more fish) and admission is free. No university offers you more than the university of angling.

4. A social good

Angling bridges generation gaps and generally is a most social activity. Angling brings people together in clubs and pubs and on the internet. This by itself is good because where people meet and chat, discuss, exchange information, argue, explain and speculate, there is a communication culture richer than the lonely silence of the TV wasteland. People meeting and talking is like a coral reef: there's colour, it vibrates life. Rarely mentioned, if at all, is the economic angle of recreational fishing. Unlike in Walton's day, there is an industry behind the pursuit of the good angling life. This industry creates employment and wealth, which is highly desirable. Anglers and industry are also an environmental force (no fish, no anglers, no industry) to be reckoned with.

5. Life joy generator

Angling isn't escapism: you never get away from it all, especially not from yourself. If anything fishing brings you back to yourself. Angling will, by virtue of the aesthetic experience, generate joy of life. Furthermore, there is surely no other pastime which involves so many concomitant pleasures. Again think of the people you meet, the stories you hear and think of food and wine, which are the key words leading us to Lutry.

Lutry is a picturesque little village on the shores of Lake Geneva, part of that famous Swiss shoreline stretching from Geneva to Montreux, where half the world's celebrities reside in style and discretion or have their offspring educated in one of the exclusive boarding schools. It's a region of great historical interest. Just think of Calvin, Dunant, Gibbon, Madame de Staël and Necker to name but a few of the people who, in one way or another, have changed the world. The terraced vineyards along the shore are part of a long-standing tradition. The part of the shore on which Lutry is located is called the Lavaux, and the locals would, not without reason, claim that the very best wine of Lake Geneva or, for that matter, anywhere else, is produced right at their front door.

Lutry is also rightly proud of its lovely promenade, where all the frightfully elegant people make you feel, in the fashion stakes, like a backwoodsman. There is a small harbour where the million-pound yacht lives in peaceful harmony with the modest fishing boat. And there is Alphonse.

Alphonse is a dedicated perch fisherman. He fishes from the pier with a paternoster rig. The lead at the tail weighs a hefty 30 grams – then in regular intervals there are four or five tinsely droppers. Alphonse is an excellent caster: that lead shoots out like a projectile, and you have great difficulty spotting the tiny splash where it hits the water. He waits till the line tightens and then starts lifting the rod high up, pointing at the sky; then he quickly lowers it, tip pointing right at the lake, and reels in and then repeats the action.

Friends of Regina's live in Lutry and had invited us for a birthday party. Although I am not one for birthday parties, I agreed to go along – after all, there might be a chance of wetting a line. Alas, my hopes were crushed when Regina put her foot down: no fishing rod in the boot this time round. The party was to start at 6:30pm and Regina reasoned from past experience that at precisely 5pm the fish would really start to take and that there was no way I would make it in time for the party. I can't say she was far off the mark; after all, fishing is infinitely more exciting than a silly birthday party. What's the next best thing to fishing? Watching somebody fishing and talking fishing, which is exactly what I did that Saturday late afternoon with Alphonse there at the pier in Lutry. Time flew and imagine my horror when I realised that I was already an hour late. I hastened back to the hotel, where I expected a furious Regina, but to my surprise I found her in the best of spirits. It turned out that she had calculated that, even without a fishing rod, I would be at least an hour late so she had simply set the party time an hour ahead. I had returned to the hotel precisely on time.

Next morning I woke early, looked out the window and saw Alphonse at the pier. As fishing conversations are never really final, I felt that there were still a few points which I would like to discuss with Alphonse. At breakfast I got leave until midday and made for the pier. There were Alphonse and a boy engaged in a conversation about pike fishing. Greetings were exchanged, Alphonse fished on, and the boy and I watched, leaning on the railings. We watched, we talked, and the boy, Nicholas, turned out to be a very keen and interested young angler of about fourteen years of age.

We chatted about this, that and the other and I asked him why he hadn't taken his fishing rod with him. He explained that he was there for the weekend for a family reunion (Saturday evening) and that his mother was adamant that no fishing rod would be taken along. Nicholas had to be at that party. Sighs of sadness underlined Nicholas's feelings as he related this to me. When I told him that my wife had taken a similarly stonehearted stance, we agreed that there was no justice in the world, but we also agreed that a sorrow shared was a sorrow halved. Sorrow turned into hilarity when Charles joined the group. There was nothing funny about Charles. In fact, he looked as though he was in a quite sombre mood. However, when it turned out that he, too, was a frustrated fisherman who had been forced into attending some party the evening before and whose wife had also banned the fishing rod, we all saw the funny side of the situation.

So there we were, Alphonse fishing with a trio of expert onlookers. Alphonse didn't mind, conversed and stayed concentrated at the same time. Fishing the pier in Lutry requires those skills. Alphonse's Sunday morning, by the way, runs according to the principle "church for her, fishing for me". Alphonse packs in at 11:30am sharp. This he manages to do because he stops fishing at 11am, that is, when the church is out. Stopping fishing means he tells himself to stop now

236

and it takes him about half an hour to actually stop. He says he can't just reel in and leave. In the busiest of places the fisherman is in communion with nature and an oasis of tranquillity. At 11.30am it is "L'heure du Pastis" – the apéritif and at 12:15 sharp he meets his wife at home. They certainly are well organised.

As the morning progressed and became warmer, Lutry's promenade got busier and busier. It was a glorious Indian summer day towards the end of the season and everybody was out enjoying the sun. There's a playground next to the pier, and the happy sounds from there mingled with bits of conversation from the people strolling along the promenade, the gently tapping waves and the hooting of the approaching passenger ships. This bouquet of sounds was further enriched by an unusual whining noise, the source of which we couldn't immediately identify. Eventually we spotted the model plane. I idly wondered about the name of the plane and for no particular reason at all named it *The Spirit of Lutry*.

Before long we also located the pilot. He was about a hundred yards down to our right on a jetty-like structure at the end of which there were two benches. It just served as a platform for those beautifully situated benches. There stood the pilot of the steering *The Spirit of Lutry* over what, in proportion to the size of the craft, seemed the ocean.

As Alphonse had enough perch for lunch, he proposed that Nicholas should try casting. He had mentioned earlier that he had never cast a 30-gram lead. Alphonse is a superb caster: he whacks that lead out in great style. Anyway, there was Alphonse, explaining to Nicholas the action in every detail and in slow motion. Then it was Nicholas's turn but he hadn't quite got the hang of it yet. So Alphonse took the rod again and gave another demonstration. Things then happened in seconds. We all saw the model seaplane approaching from the right on a direct collision course. As it happened, the lead smashed the tail of the plane. It flew on for a second or two and then started spinning and crashed into the water.

While this was happening, the lead followed its course and splashed into the lake far beyond the scene of the crash. We were dumbfounded, but more was to follow: Alphonse, though watching

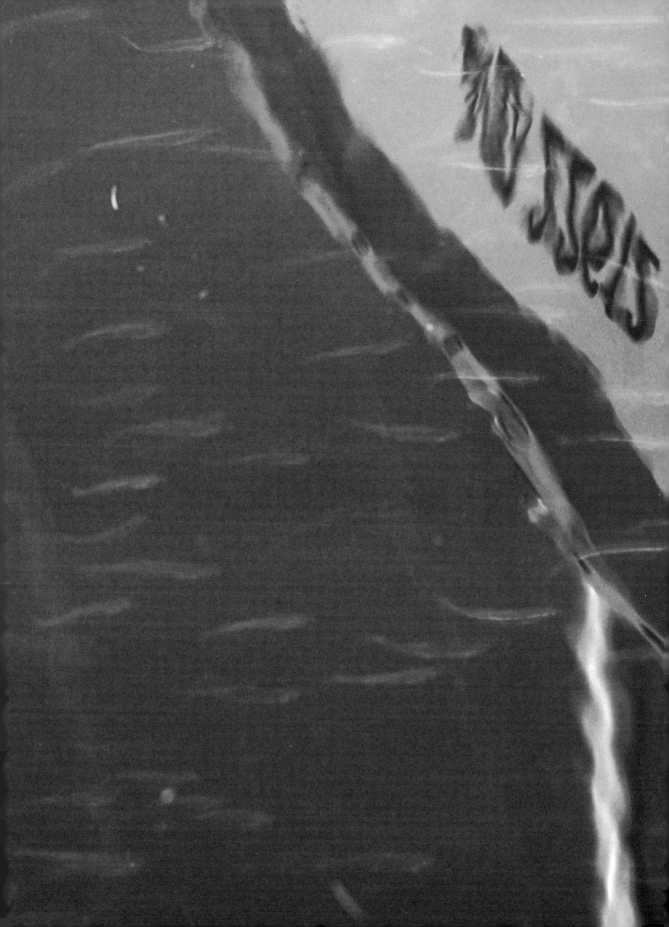

the scene of the crash, routinely went through the motions and —
would you believe it?— hooked a pike! Of course, the focus of our
attention shifted immediately to Alphonse and the pike, forgetting
about the poor pilot who must have been as stunned as we were. He
couldn't possibly have seen the cause of the crash because from that
distance looking into the sun you simply don't see the monofilament
or the lead.

Alphonse landed a beautiful eight-pounder and as it was
approaching 11:30am, he invited us for an apéritif. The pike was put
into Alphonse's fish bag and we proceeded to the Café de la Plage.
Now guess who was sitting next to the only available table with the
controls in front of him? None other than the hapless pilot, along
with two friends. As they didn't know that "we" were the cause of the
crash, they didn't take any notice of us or of a certain embarrassment
which had taken hold of us.

The pilot, a young man of about eighteen, radiated intelligence,
nobleness, manners, style and wealth, as only Indians can do. His
two friends looked European—they were probably all boarders
in one of those famous schools. They conversed in French and
we couldn't help listening. From what I could overhear, the plane
was apparently a self-developed high-tech miracle full of intricate
electronic novelties controlled by self-programmed software. The
pilot was clearly scientifically minded: he didn't regret so much the
loss as such, but the fact that he didn't know what had caused the
loss. In other words, what was really nagging him was the question
as to where he had made a mistake, where it had gone wrong. The
plane was lost in the ocean and there was no way he was ever going
to know. The sincerity in the words of the young man was probably
the reason why Alphonse turned round and addressed the pilot with
the words: "I downed your plane."

Silence.

It was broken by the pilot, who simply asked, "But how?". The
"how" expressed that he had already accepted that there couldn't
be a "Why?" Alphonse explained, and the three young men couldn't
hide their incredulity. They probably thought Alphonse was having
them on. Only when Alphonse showed them the 30-gram lead and

when we confirmed Alphonse's story did the disbelief slowly give way to amazement. A mobile phone rang. It was the pilot's, and after glancing at the caller's number, he took the call. He changed into a language we didn't understand, so we continued to explain the accident to the pilot's friends and also showed them the pike. The pilot rang off and rejoined the conversation, relating that the caller had been his father and that he was greatly amused by the accident. His father, the pilot added, was also a fisherman. Spontaneously I asked, "Where does your father fish?" "In Waterville, Ireland" came the reply without hesitation. I was thunderstruck for a moment—it's a small world as the saying goes, but that small?

It was truly miraculous. Mathematicians will of course protest that there is nothing miraculous about it, but that doesn't mar the enjoyment of the surprise in the least. That young man was the son of the mysterious Indian prince in Waterville—so there really is an Indian prince fishing in Waterville! I had always thought the Indian prince was fiction invented by the ghillies. I distinctly remember

241

asking Michael who the prince was and Michael giving me the truthful answer "Well, he is an Indian prince and an excellent fisherman". I never saw the prince or any person who could have been him. It seemed to me that whenever there was a blank day all round, one of the ghillies would come into *The Lobster* and say, "The prince got one" signifying nobody could catch fish on a day like that except a mysterious prince with superhuman piscatorial qualities. I always took the Indian prince for a standing joke, but my Irish friends had stuck strictly to fact – and I thought they were giving me pure fiction.

Explaining this took time, so all the anglers were running late. Suddenly we were besieged by Nicolas's mother and three wives who had run out of patience at the same moment, looked for the missing anglers and found us. A potentially uncomfortable situation was in the air: mothers and wives can be very unsympathetic. Our new friends rose to the occasion and saved the day brilliantly. With their impeccable French, their spruce attire, their polished manners and fantastic diplomatic skills, they wooed the ladies to join us. Any female antagonism there might have been melted away in seconds under the delightful fireworks of charm and attention given to them by the young princes (I decided they were surely all princes).

I can't remember who suggested that we should all have lunch together at the hotel *Le Rivage*, but the idea was enthusiastically welcomed by everyone. A few mobile phone calls later, we all gently strolled over to the terrace of *Le Rivage*. The chef came out in person to take the pike and the perch and told us how he intended to prepare them. The meal turned out to be a supreme culinary event, and the mood of the party was animated, cordial, relaxed and stimulating.

In that unique crystal-clear, golden-tinged early autumn light, we celebrated angling, life and beauty.

242

Well, Jim, that's all for the moment. I hope this will be of some help to you. If you have any questions or need more information, don't hesitate to contact me at my website *www.philosofish.ch*

I hope to see you here next summer.

Love,
Alex.

Send Chat Attach Address Fonts Colors Save As Draft

To: alex@philosofish.ch

Cc:

Subject: fishing

Dear Alex

Thanks a lot. It's a bit late, actually. And a lot longer than I expected (my deadline was a year ago). But thanks anyway.

Love,
Jim

Bibliography

In my view, still the most important book on angling is Izaak Walton's unsurpassed *The Compleat Angler*. The Ecco Press edition features a perspicacious and thoughtful introduction by Thomas McGuane.

The Compleat Angler, Izaak Walton, The Ecco Press, 1995, Hopewell, New Jersey (USA) and Ontario (Canada), ISBN 0-88001-406-7, (15, 39-41, 52, 104, 114, 125, 144, 183–185, 196)

Fishing and Thinking, like *The Compleat Angler* is a book you can read time and again; it never ceases to surprise and inspire.

Fishing and Thinking, A.A. Luce, Swan Hill Press, Shrewsbury, England, 1990, ISBN 1 85310 151 6

Bryn Hammond's seminal and pioneering *Halcyon Days* is a landmark in angling literature and culture. It completes my list of the three most important books on angling.

Halcyon Days, Bryn Hammond, Swan Hill Press, Shrewsbury, England, 1992, ISBN 1 85310 153 2, (4-5, 10–11)

Once a Flyfisher, Laurence Catlow, Merlin Unwin Books, Ludlow, England, ISBN 1-873674-48-1, (251)

Angling in Art, Tom Quinn, The Sportsman's Press, London, 1991, ISBN 0-948253-55-X, (23)

Jerusalem Creek, Ted Leeson, The Lyons Press, Guilford, Connecticut, 2002, ISBN 1-58574-554-5, (57)

Sea Trout Fishing, Hugh Falkus, H.F. & G. Witherby Ltd., 1983, ISBN 0 85493 115 5, (112-113)

The Float, Keith Harwood, The Medlar Press Ltd., Ellesmere, England, 2003, ISBN 1899 600 25 6, (167)

Haunted by Waters – Fly Fishing in North American Literature, Mark Browning, Ohio University Press, 1998, ISBN 0-8214-1218-3, (26-27, 32)

The quotations from Roland Pertwee and A.J. McClane are taken from:

Fisherman's Bounty, Ed. Nick Lyons, Simon & Schuster, New York, 1988, ISBN 0-671-65745-3, (28, 321)

The Pocket Guide to Fishing Knots, Peter Owen, Merlin Unwin Books, Ludlow, England, 2003, ISBN 1 873674 34 1, (9)

Hook, Line and Thinker – Angling and Ethics, Alexander Schwab, Merlin Unwin Books, 2003, Ludlow, England, ISBN 1 873674 59 7

The History and Science of Knots, JC Turner and P. van de Griend Eds., World Scientific Publishing Ltd., Singapore, 1995, ISBN 9810224699

Messages from Water, Masaru Emoto, HADO Kyoikusha, Tokyo
This is the most beautiful angling book there is. The poet and the photographer are both anglers and it shows. This book is about the beauty of angling, the beauty of nature – about perfection.

River, Poems by Ted Hughes, photographs by Peter Keen, Faber and Faber, London, 1983, ISBN 0-571-13088-7, (120–124)

Poetry in the making, Ted Hughes, Faber & Faber, London, 1969, ISBN 0 571 09076 1, (60-61)

The Cosmic Serpent, Jeremy Narby, published by Phoenix, London, 1999, ISBN 0 75380 851 X, (102)

Mayflies, Richard Wilbur, Harcourt Inc., New York, 2000, ISBN 0-15-100469-2, (17)

The Water Wizard, The Extraordinary Properties of Natural Water, Viktor Schauberger (translated and edited by Callum Coats) Gill & Macmillan Ltd., Dublin, 1997, ISBN 1 85860 049 9, (15-16)

Texte zur Grundlegung der Ästhetik, A.G. Baumgarten, Felix Meiner Verlag, Hamburg, 1983, ISBN 3-7873-0573-4, (79)

More bibliographical information is available at

www.philosofish.ch

List of photographs

One of the key contentions in this book is that, sooner or later, you'll discover beauty at the heart of all angling matters. It follows that even the bleakest of angling scenes must somehow have beauty, or at least aesthetic appeal, in them – and this is what I have tried to prove with the pictures in this book. The choice of photos follows the themes in the argument: e.g. the aesthetic experience of concentrating, of sharing knowledge, of finding beauty in unexpected places (knots), beauty in the minutiae of fishing equipment, in fish scales, etc. However, none of the angling scenes was staged. I personally know only three (including Jim) of the anglers featured and I didn't know who I was going to meet and where precisely I would meet them. Again the assumption was that this didn't matter because regardless of circumstances there is always beauty to be discovered. This also meant that there would be no retakes (except for static indoor subjects). So what you see is a real-life documentary of the beauty of angling rather than staged beauty over a period of, say, half a year. But of course these photos only show half the picture, because beauty isn't just visual. There is the rhythm of the waves tapping on the side of the boat, the smell of grass after rain, the feel of the wind burning your cheeks with cold, and a thousand and one other sensations. Nevertheless, I hope that some of these pictures will remind you of an experience of beauty, or stimulate you to go fishing once again, to go out and to look at the beauty of it all.

Page 8
Location: Brussels, Belgium
Subject: Jim. Photographed by his father Yves Goossens Bara.

Page 11
Location: Waterville, Ireland
Subject: Pub sign of *The Lobster* in Waterville.

Pages 14/15
Location: Lough Currane, Ireland
Subject: Approaching squall. Waterscape, beauty of nature.

Page 22
Location: Lake Thun, Switzerland
Subject: Cormorants. Understanding fellow-fishers and what they do. Learning about nature.

Page 29
Location: Lough Currane, Ireland
Subject: Michael O'Sullivan

Page 36
Location: Indoors
Subject: Beauty of the hook. Proportion, function, finish.

Page 36
Location: On the mount
Subject: Microscopic algae. They were around in the stone age (and way before that) as they are now. Everything in and around water is of interest to the angler.

Page 38
Location: Lake Geneva, Lutry, Switzerland
Subject: Fisherman's shadow. The fishing gesture is universally recognized.

Page 47
Location: Waterville, Ireland
Subject: Cummeragh River. Meandering river, continuity and change.

Page 49
Location: Tackle Shop Bernhard, Wichtrach, Switzerland
Subject: The rod rack, the Milky Way of rod rings.

Page 53
Location: Lake Thun, Switzerland
Subject: Mayfly. Ephemeral beauty in nature. Symmetry, harmony. Transitory yet eternal.

Page 57
Location: Desroches Island, Seychelles
Subject : Cookie II. Stage set for the story of the abominable Duc de X.

Page 59
Location: Ivy House Lakes, Grittenham (Wilts), England
Subject: No fishing sign.

Page 63
Location: Lough Currane, Ireland
Subject: Salmon. A closer look at the familiar often reveals beauty.

Page 64/65
Location: Indoors
Subject: Reconstruction of the tangle the Japanese angler disentangled.

Page 69
Location: Lake Thun, Switzerland
Subject: Tangle. What a beauty! Almost a pity to disentangle it.

Page 73
Location: Indoors
Subject: A good knot looks good.

Page 75
Location: Indoors
Subject: Transparent monofilament.

Page 76
Location: Lake Oeschinen, Kandersteg, Switzerland
Subject: The quest for beauty. Ice fishing. Fisherman making his way across the lake.

Page 79
Location: Lake Thun, Switzerland
Subject: Whitefish scales floating in clear water after cleaning fish.
A galaxy of scales.

Page 80
Location: Lake Thun, Switzerland
Subject: Fishing for whitefish the traditional way. Again the fishing gesture is universally recognised.

Page 84
Location: River Aare between Thun and Bern, Switzerland
Subject: Grayling angler. Beauty of scenery and light. At one with nature.

Page 89
Location: Lake Thun, Switzerland
Subject: Boy showing whitefish he caught, the joy of achievement.

Page 95
Location: Lake Thun, Switzerland
Subject: Heavy rain. The Milky Way of rain drops.

Page 99
Location: Tackle Shop Bernhard, Wichtrach, Switzerland
Subject: Trout sculpture in the car park.

Page 101
Location: Trout pond, Kräiligen, Switzerland
Subject : Achievement!

Pages 102/103
Location: Lake Thun, Switzerland
Subject: A fine summer day. Angling is fun.

Page 104
Location: Waterville House, Waterville, Ireland
Subject: The wholesome nature of possession of a quarry; and pride in catch.
Porcelain angler.

Page 106/107
Location: Ivy House Lakes, Grittenham (Wilts), England
Subject: Bait. Breeding maggots requires know-how. No fish is as good as the one caught with your self-bred maggots (or self-tied flies). To the breeder this a beautiful sight. And there is something in that mass of maggots which is fascinating.

Page 111
Location: Tackle Shop Bernhard, Wichtrach, Switzerland
Subject: Bait. Zulus in the tackle shop. There is something mesmeric about the quantity; and the ribbings shine like little stars.

Page 113
Location: Loch Ailsh, Scotland
Subject: Water. Rhythm, harmony.

Page 116
Location: Tackle Shop Bernhard, Wichtrach, Switzerland
Subject: Salmon eggs.

Page 119
Location: River Aare in Thun, Switzerland
Subject: Vortex. Water not so much a liquid as a body. "Landscapes" on water. Quite extraordinary once you start looking for them.

Page 123
Location: Lake Thun, Switzerland
Subject: Beautifully shaped whitefish.

Page 125
Location: Lough Currane, Ireland
Subject: Waterscape.

Page 129
Location: River Aare between Thun and Bern, Switzerland
Subject: Concentration of a grayling angler.

Page 131
Location: Lake Thun, Switzerland
Subject: Detail of centre pin reel. Beauty in familiar objects.

Page 135
Location: My fly tying corner
Subject: The beauty of fly tying. Even if it's fairly wild looking, it's your own fly.

Page 136
Location: My fly tying corner
Subject: Fish eyes for lures. Symmetry, harmony, rhythm.

Page 141
Location: Ivy House Lakes, Grittenham (Wilts.), England
Subject: Competition angler. Expectation, concentration, focus.

Page 145
Location: Zwingsee, Inzell, Bavaria, Germany
Subject: Trout and fly. Expectation, concentration, focus.

Page 146
Location: Lough Currane, Ireland
Subject: Rain drop. Harmony, symmetry, connection.

Page 151
Location: Trout pond, Kräiligen, Switzerland
Subject: Concentration, determination, skill.

Page 153
Location: River Rhône, Geneva, Switzerland
Subject: Fishing with the wooden frame. Balance, skill, tradition.

Page 155
Location: River Aare in Thun, Switzerland
Subject: Young urban angler in urban style. A pursuit sans frontières.

Page 157
Location: Tackle Shop Bernhard, Wichtrach, Switzerland
Subject: Floats. Aesthetic pleasure in familiar objects.

Page 158
Location: Beau Vallon Beach, Mahé, Seychelles
Subject : Storm clearing. Beauty in water and light.

Page 161
Location: Lough Currane, Ireland
Subject: Rod and line mirrored in water. Spiral shape. Meandering.

Page 163
Location; Lake Thun, Switzerland
Subject: Float and stars (sunny day and little waves). Again water as a body not as liquid.

Page 165
Location: Ivy House Lakes, Grittenham (Wilts.), England
Subject: Angler merging into surroundings. Patience. Beauty in light and structures. The angler belongs there.

Page 167
Location: River Aare, between Thun and Bern, Switzerland
Subject: Grayling. Marvellous rhythm and symmetry in the scales.

Page 169
Location: Tackle Shop Bernhard, Wichtrach, Switzerland
Subject: Lures. Tempting, shiny, appealing objects.

Page 171
Location: Lough Currane, Morgan's Rock, Ireland
Subject: Refreshment. Even here water looks more solid than liquid.

Page 174
Location: River Aare in Thun, Switzerland
Subject: Young urban angler. Although the setting might not look appealing, the river the young angler fishes is crystal clear. He is at home here. Also a picture of determination and perseverance: it was brass monkeys.

Page 177
Location: Tackle Shop Bernhard, Wichtrach, Switzerland
Subject: Landing net. Anglers need to be watchful to evade the net of political correctness.

Page 179
Location: Zwingsee, Inzell, Bavaria, Germany
Subject: Sunlight and water playing on a sturgeon's tail fin. Picture taken from the bank into the clear water.

Page 181
Location: Trout pond, Kräiligen, Switzerland
Subject : Focusing, concentration, expectation.

Page 183
Location: In our garden
Subject: Inside rear view of a salmon's head. Symmetry, waves and vortex.

Page 185
Location: Ivy House Lakes, Grittenham (Wilts.), England
Subject: Granny trimming a knot the traditional way.

Page 187
Location: At home
Subject: Food.

Page 188
Location: Café de la Poste, Lutry, Switzerland
Subject: Boned perch.

Page 191
Location: Ivy House Lakes, Grittenham (Wilts), England
Subject: Anglers enjoying a cup of tea.

Page 193
Location: Café de la Poste, Lutry, Switzerland
Subject : Spines of the boned perch. They were absolutely delicious.

Page 196/197
Location: Lough Currane, Ireland
Subject: Dead calm with "ripples of hope".

Page 201
Location: Waterville, Ireland
Subject: Inside Michael's fishing hut. The order in things isn't always obvious.

Page 203
Location: In our garden
Subject: Aesthetic appeal of a feather (golden pheasant tippets). Symmetry, harmony. There's no doubt something Japanese about this feather.

Page 205
Location: In our kitchen
Subject: Salmon in the pan. Symmetry, harmony of the "drawings".

Page 206
Location: My fly tying corner
Subject: Hackle. Symmetry.

Page 209
Location: Zwingsee, Inzell, Bavaria, Germany
Subject: Damsel. The beauty in the detail.

Page 211
Location: Ivy House Lakes, Grittenham (Wilts), England
Subject: Pleasure. Reflection or just relaxing?

Page 213
Location: Ivy House Lakes, Grittenham (Wilts.), England
Subject: Concentration.

Page 215
Location: Lough Currane, Ireland
Subject: Harmony, tranquillity. The two boats somehow belong there. Everything is "naturally" in proportion.

Page 217
Location: My fly tying corner
Subject: Fly-tying.

Page 219
Location: River Aare in Thun
Subject: Fish eating bird. Merganser, adult female. Another interesting "colleague". The glass-like quality of the water is just beautiful.

Page 220/221
Location: Lake Thun, Switzerland
Subject: Anglers with dog.

Page 223
Location: Indoors
Subject: Rod ring, spiral shapes. Beautiful evocative object for all anglers.

Page 225
Location: Ivy House Lakes, Grittenham (Wilts), England
Subject: Icebreaker. Two forms of water. Beauty in light.